The Marriage Pioneers

The Marriage Pioneers

Three Timeless Strengths for Today's Marriages

Interviews with

Dr. David and Dr. Vera Mace

by

Dr. Britton and Dr. Bobbye Wood

The Marriage Pioneers

Published by Clovercroft Publishing, Franklin, Tennessee

Photos shared courtesy of:
Ron Musgrave
Fiona Mace Patterson
Haley Nicas
Rachel and Chad Eskew
Britton Wood

Copy Edit by Lapiz Digital Services

Cover and Interior Design by Adept Content Solutions

Printed in the United States of America

978-1-949572-24-7

Contents

In loving memory of
David and Vera Mace
For their Courage and Resolution
In giving of themselves to couples around the world, which includes us.

Introduction to the Purpose and Concept of the Book

Introduction to David and Vera Mace

In the 1930s, families across the world were trying to survive physically and financially, with all countries in the grip of economic issues so severe that even today the time is referred to as The Great Depression. Growing the marriage relationship was not on anyone's top priority list. Those who were concerned about that relationship at all (even the church, which conducted more than fifty percent of all marriages) simply expected couples to stay married no matter what their quality of life. By the end of the decade, both church and state had much more immediate issues to deal with, life-threatening and economically catastrophic.

Yet, one couple, David and Vera Mace of London, England, decided from the outset of their marriage in 1933 that their life goal would be improving the quality of family life. The best way to accomplish this, they boldly stated at the beginning of their long and illustrious careers, was "to focus on the heart of the home, the couple." David and Vera recognized even then that a healthy marriage relationship was central to healthy family dynamics and sought ways to strengthen couples.

At the time, David and Vera began their life work, there were few books about marriage in existence; there was no research on how to make the marriage relationship go well, no organizations providing aid to couples in trouble, no money available for those who wanted to concentrate on growth for couples, and certainly no go-to places for couples to learn to relate in healthy ways.

So, as the Depression deepened, and in England, the storm clouds gathered that would soon become World War II (WWII), in 1938 The Marriage Guidance Council was formed, with volunteer counselors working with David and Vera in the world's first effort to address the fact that marriage could and should lead to personal and relational growth. This endeavor makes David and Vera *true marriage pioneers.*

After the war when the family was once again united in England (Vera had taken their two daughters to safety in the US), the Maces once again began "arming" themselves for a very different war: an all-out assault to gain funds and recognition for the Marriage Guidance Council and for their goal of building strengths in families through improving the relational health of the married couple.

Across the UK, David and Vera began persuading a team of professionals—governmental officials with defined human services roles, key leaders with ties to the King, the Church, and to academia—to join them, making a combination able to exert enough influence to make a difference for marriages and families across England.

It was such a success that the London Marriage Guidance Council proliferated and soon was duplicated in many countries, causing David to divide his time between his country and the many cultures who embraced the new Mace philosophies and formed various organizations to aid couples. Now the world was acknowledging David and Vera as *true marriage pioneers.*

Then the Maces embarked on studying marriages worldwide, traveling to seventy-nine different cultures, tribes, and venues in order to amass the data to back up what they suspected all along—marriages across the world needed help and the Maces were able to provide that assistance. This was yet another way that David and Vera emerged as *true marriage pioneers.*

In the late 1940s, the Mace family settled in the US, where David began several university and medical school posts. They began to write books about the marriage customs they encountered in their world travels (some thirty-three in all translated into eleven different languages) and to find organizations that could address detrimental issues facing marriages, which they knew from their worldwide research to be universal. In the succeeding decades, they received many awards and honors for their work as *true marriage pioneers,* including the Year of the Family Patron Award given by the United Nations.

The Purpose and the Format

In the middle of the decade of the 1970s, Bobbye and Britton Wood first heard David and Vera speak about their ideas concerning the importance of a quality marriage relationship and how to get it. It happened at a workshop introducing the Maces to Texas and to a group of couples who might be interested in their unique ideas and philosophies.

The Woods at that time was a two-career family with three young daughters. Like many couples, what the Woods desired was more joy and satisfaction in their everyday relationship; what they lacked was a specific direction that would provide it. What they wanted was a better connection both with themselves and with each other in the midst of a fast-paced and complex world. What they needed was a relational Global Positioning System (GPS) that explained how to find and expand that connection. *What the Maces did was to provide that direction.*

In the two-day workshop the Maces showed couples:

- how to focus on where they are in their relationship;
- how to realistically assess what each of them wants to achieve, both for themselves and for their relationship; and
- how to create a workable plan for getting there, with specific skills to implement the plan.

The skills were simple but effective, and couples learned that using those skills quickly led to an increased awareness of an essential triangle for growth and connection: self, partner, and the relationship that holds them together. Today many counselors and marriage educators refer to that triangle as the "you," the "me," and the "us," but at that time in history, it was a new and untried concept for most couples. In the Maces' philosophy, all three sides of this triangle must be considered for the ultimate satisfaction of the couple to be achieved.

In this short time with the Maces, the trajectory of Bobbye's and Britton's marriage was changed, for they saw a life focus that they believed in. What followed was a training program in the Maces' philosophies and techniques and then a week of interviews with the Maces at their mountain house in Black Mountain, North Carolina.

There, for five wonderful days they learned more about the keywords and specific skills the Maces recommended and how they came to design those skills as they studied marriages around the world. For Bobbye and Britton, they were five days of discovery, laughter, education, insight, inspiration, instruction, and hope. David and Vera's life work proved to transcend time—ideals and skills applicable today as much as they were in the 1930s.

With the practical skills that David and Vera recommend, any couple at any stage of life's journey can access the goals they want to achieve (both for themselves and for their relationship). This is a system unrelated to age, economics, education, or culture. It is for:

- Newly weds who want to get off to a good start.
- Typical goal-setting young adults who expect each other to take meeting goals seriously.
- Stretched and stressed couples hoping for some new ideas to add spice to their daily interactions and to change old, ineffective habits and patterns.
- Two-career, time-challenged couples with busy lives, children, and few uninterrupted hours.

- Retired couples looking for deeper companionship and closeness.

Over the years in the back of their memories, Bobbye and Britton wanted the world to hear directly from David and Vera's voices as the *true marriage pioneers*. Therefore, the thirty compact disks have been transcribed into a book in interview form, as David and Vera's ideals and philosophies emerge, along with the voices of Bobbye and Britton, as they respond from their perspectives and add ideas from current marriage experts. The book's format will be, as David himself put it, "one relationship interrogating another relationship about the relationship."

The following excerpt shows the basic format for the illustration of the Maces' main ideas:

> ***Britton:*** I am sure over the years that you have been asked many times, "What's the secret to a happy marriage?" How do you respond to that?
>
> ***David:*** WITH GREAT ANNOYANCE! Because it is trying to reduce relationship down to ONE idea, to ONE task—and that can't be done. There is a whole regimen of ideas and tasks. There is a lot of work and planning involved, and the goals would be different for individual couples.
>
> ***Vera:*** Yes, every couple is unique, so every couple must decide together what it is they most want to accomplish in their relationship. No one can decide it for them. Then they need to start practicing the skills faithfully, and the rewards suggest that the skills lead to connection, growth, intimacy, and family harmony.
>
> ***David:*** *There is no easy way to accomplish a good marriage.* You can cut the corners if you want to, but if you want a good marriage, you have to pay the price for it just as you would for any other important goal that you want to achieve.

But the fact is that none of this is a "secret" any longer. It might have been at one time, and that is a tragedy. I think that until now those who failed in marriage were not failures but victims. But now information is becoming available from many sources that can help couples. What we want to do is put it into the hands of as many couples as possible and to challenge them to use that information to build health and joy in their own relationships.

The really exciting thing to us is the number of couples who may be needing just the things that we are talking about with you. We quite like this interview idea of yours for introducing our basic ideas for helping marriages to thrive.

We never expected to make money on our discoveries about healthy marriage and just hoped that it could have a good effect on society in general. That those discoveries have been well received is very heartening to us. We enjoy all our awards and affirmations, but it is the couples like you two who have been inspired that are our real reward. We hope that this book will be part of the inspiration.

Bobbye: As do we.

In addition to the interviews with David and Vera, in each chapter Bobbye and Britton will add a real-life experience of their own concerning the subject being discussed in that chapter, drawing from their own travels speaking to couples in many countries and from their own interactions.

Each chapter will also include an exercise that a couple can do together. The exercises are designed to give each person an opportunity to share both his or her ideas and opinions on both the skills being discussed and to actually use those skills. The purpose of the exercises is to build connection and closeness within the relationship.

Chapters will be clustered around the three strengths (or what some call the "essentials"). The Maces called those strengths The

Primary Coping System, which formed the heart of their main philosophy. The three strengths are:

1. Designing *A Mutual Commitment to Growth.*
2. Developing *A Communication Style that Works* for each couple to build understanding and closeness.
3. Practicing *A Creative Use of Conflict.*

We know that using these profound strengths build, over time, the warmth and sense of closeness that all couples dream of having when they decide to marry. Today, we marvel over the enthusiastic energy generated just by being in the presence of the other. It is an energy that Britton describes as "like newly-weds, with skills." We are now at the point of celebrating our sixty-second Anniversary, and it is with best wishes and hopes for success that we recommend these skills straight from *the true marriage pioneers.*

Strength 1

A Mutual Commitment to Growth

Identifying the Strength and Introducing the First Section

Two cups with the silhouettes of David and Vera were gifts during the Mace Phonathon to encourage Daily Couple Talk.

Chapter 1

The Philosophy of the Mutual Commitment to Growth

The meaning of human life is found in loving relationships. That is a person's deep anchorage, and one of humanity's most basic needs. Nothing is more central than this: that loving relationships can redeem and that they can sustain us in life's most difficult struggles. (David Mace's statement to the Woods during the interview process.)

One of the main reasons for writing this book is to allow the interviews with the Maces to convey their profound awareness regarding what leads to a quality relationship. The philosophy of the Mutual Commitment to Growth would call for each unique couple to set individual goals and together to set goals for their own couple growth in intimacy and shared closeness. Here is a suggestion of the origin of the pioneer philosophy that opens the "door" to new ideas concerning relationship:

Bobbye: This first principle of Marriage Enrichment—this commitment to growth—where did that come from? Did you just make it up or did it come out of your experiences in some way?

David: In our early days of marriage, expectations concerning marriage were much different. Vera and I entered marriage with much deep enthusiasm, but we were baffled by the many differences between us and the tensions they created. It was a different day from now, as I said, and there was very little in our cultural environment in the way of help or even suggestions concerning what couples need.

I re-read the books I had studied as I began my career, and these were by the outstanding authors and teachers of the time. I was puzzled to find that there was not much in those books on the importance of communication, not much on the positive role of conflict, and zero on growth as a goal for couples. We floundered like many couples until we came to some very specific ideas that we could use.

Vera: We gradually came to see that growth could happen if we both wanted it, and we looked for those ways that worked for us. We just came to the point where we saw growth—growth as individuals and growth as a couple—as something we needed. We knew that there had to be more than both of us were experiencing, and we reached out to each other to find it.

David: Yes, and for us, it was an initial painful experience where we opened up our feelings, but it cleared out a lot of extraneous "stuff" that both of us had avoided expressing. Then when that was done, it was just a matter of sustaining the good feelings produced by at last getting down to stating to each other what we both wanted.

We had of course known all along what we wanted and even perhaps what we needed. But we had somehow mistakenly assumed the other person did not want to know. When we could be candid with each other, we were both amazed at the experience.

Britton: And from this initial experience you developed the Mutual Commitment to Growth idea?

David: Basically, yes. It's important that a couple is involved in marital growth. Sharing with each other what you really want is a good place to begin. Of course, from our own experience, we did not immediately form the philosophy which eventually evolved, but the seeds for that philosophy were definitely there. Start with a desire for growth, individually and relationally, and that gives a direction for other important things.

The important thing is to keep a perspective on why you are doing this, what you will accomplish in the way of a close and connected relationship that simply cannot be achieved without attentiveness and effort during life's ever-changing surface. But when both partners can make a commitment to each other that growth will be the goal, a "door" opens that leads to exciting new vistas.

The meaning of human life is found in loving relationships. That is a person's deep anchorage, and one of humanity's most basic needs. Nothing is more central than this: that loving relationships can redeem and that they can sustain us in life's most difficult struggles.

The Mutual Commitment to Growth is the Maces' challenge to couples who have bought into the old concept that nothing you can do will change your marital relationship for the better. Your options for the future, this skeptical notion says, are to accept the *status quo* or to divorce.

The Maces referred to the Mutual Commitment to Growth as the "door" that opens a view of the kind of dynamic future potentially available to each couple who goes through it. Going through the "door" toward a more intimate future does not rely on education, economics, age, or circumstances. It relies on motivation. It relies on willingness. It relies on a hope that together each couple can custom-make the kind of marital enjoyment that each desires.

Abraham Lincoln was once criticized for being too nice to his enemies. "You should punish them. You should get rid of them," he was advised. Lincoln asked, "Do I not get rid of my enemies when I make them my friends?"

"Making friends" with a new way to look at marriage can be immediately rewarding, giving the impetus for keeping the relationship fresh. Looking at marriage in a new way may also require a change toward some relational "enemies" and unprofitable habits, such as:

- apathy about making requested changes;
- reluctance to listen;
- negative attitudes of "I'll change if you. . .";
- failure to keep promises or bargains;
- avoidance of spending adequate time designing goals;
- withholding needed information;
- a desire and need always to be the one who is "right";
- maintaining old resentments and grudges;
- failing to express gratitude when a requested change is made; and
- making assumptions about your partner's statements based on past experiences.

Making new relational "friends" sometimes requires time in order to adjust to a different perspective or attitude. But when both partners commit to the idea that they can custom-make their marriage, it opens the "door" to a myriad of possibilities that can amaze them both.

They do not have to be bound by the rules and habits of their families-of-origin. They do not have to be "like" any other couple. They soon accept the fact that like snowflakes and DNA, each couple is unique and must find the rhythms and rules that fit for them.

Sometimes a decision to try a new approach comes out of unhappiness or even alarm. Several years ago, Britton and Bobbye were speaking on Marriage Enrichment for several weeks at an international church in Madrid, Spain. They learned that the Ethiopians and Eritreans in the church family would not attend the same Bible study together because of old animosities between the two countries, animosities occurring decades earlier and having nothing to do with their current lives in Spain.

But the trends of the families from the two countries were similar, in which both Ethiopians and Eritreans were encountering disastrous family break-ups and upheavals. Couples who had known each other for years were divorcing. Children were often the victims of the chaos in the family, due to the issues of the parents. It was a subject of great concern to both ethnic groups.

So, for one evening, motivated by those important and heartfelt issues, the two groups came together for a night of Marriage Enrichment just to see if it offered any insights that they might use in their own families. Even grandparents attended, hoping for information that might be helpful in the family difficulties that they were experiencing.

The groups sat on opposite sides of the room, each group with its own translator. But the couples came, they stayed, they listened, they asked questions through their translators, and they participated in simple couple exercises on the value of a happy marriage. Families worked together on growth and how to get it. Grandparents contributed their knowledge, and everyone knew this was an important occasion.

Many months later after the Woods had left Spain and returned to their home, they learned from the pastor of the church that the two groups had begun to meet to discuss their issues. Families had discovered that there might be a few things they could do, as motivated and concerned church members, to prevent the divorces and resultant family trauma they had been experiencing.

We learned that there was even a discussion concerning putting the two international groups together for Bible study. It was exciting news for these communities and for the church. And it began with couples discussing together their hearts' concerns and making simple plans for improving their marriage and family life. It may all have come out of the deep alarm about what was happening to them, but once they looked through the "door" to view the future, they saw that growth was not only needed but also possible.

The Woods' Experience with the Mutual Commitment to Growth

The Woods heartily endorse the idea that the goal-setting required by the Mutual Commitment to Growth can lead to exciting new accomplishments. It is a commitment which can offer the motivation and spur the efforts for trying out new skills and working on needed changes. The Woods have used it over the decades since the time they first heard the Maces speak.

For instance, the time was approaching for the celebration of their sixtieth wedding anniversary, so they made a list of Sixty Sensational Things they would like to do during that year. The goals were worth achieving and celebrating. The only rule for what went on the list was that both persons had to find it sensational. That shortened the list somewhat, but still the discussion of the goals continued.

It was a list of interest to both children and grandchildren, who often called to inquire about it. "How many things do you have now?" they frequently asked. Then during the year, the questions changed to "How many of the things have you done?" and "What do you have left to do?" It seemed to the Woods as the months went by, the family was proud of a couple who took their marriage seriously and selected some specific goals for celebration.

A few of the items on the list were costly, such as taking country/western dance lessons, traveling to visit all grandchildren, going to the Texas Rangers Baseball Team's spring training in Arizona, and taking a trip with each daughter and her spouse. But spaced out over such an important year, the money did not seem to be a prohibitive factor, and energy often came from working through the list. Also, many of the goals cost nothing, such as playing dominoes every day, taking walks together, and working on jigsaw puzzles.

Britton introduced the goal of The Triple S, which he said stood for Sensational Sex for Seniors, and Bobbye agreed. Apparently, it was a popular item, for as Bobbye kept a tally on a calendar, they discovered at the end of the year they had accomplished this goal over 320 times.

The Sixty Sensational Things was just a list—a way to celebrate a milestone, an achievement both the Woods and their family were proud of. Celebrations are often needed for couples stressed and stretched with job, family, and duties, but the celebrations will more than likely not happen without some initial planning.

There can be Five Fabulous Things or Twenty-Four Terrific Things, wherever you are on life's journey. The Mutual Commitment to Growth provides the format, the "door," to new and enriching vistas within the relationship.

Couple Exercise

The couple exercise is simple. It is to make a Growth Plan.

Start with a conversation about the good things in your relationship, the things you appreciate and count on. Positive conversations serve as a helpful starting point and make things easier.

Get two blank sheets of paper. Each partner will write down any goal of importance. Include some personal goals, some goals that show support for your partner, and some specific couple goals. Here is a mini-version of what it might look like.

The Marital Growth Plan **Date________**

I want for me

I want for you

I want for us

Each partner now has a list. Share them, talk about strategies for achieving the goals, and you have begun.

Even if you are only thinking about this plan today, go back and fill it in later. Perhaps the former NFL Football player Emmitt Smith is right when he said that if we only think about but do not write down our goals or say them out loud to someone, they are only dreams. They are easily forgotten under the pressure of the everyday. When we write them down or speak them, they become goals, and we have a better chance to work toward achieving them. Others can even help us with our goals. Emmitt Smith was so convinced of this fact that he kept his goals taped to his bathroom mirror just to keep them in mind every day.

Be sure to celebrate the accomplishments of your goals—both individual and couple. Celebrations are always needed and help both partners see that this is an important undertaking.

These two papers are flexible documents. Keep reviewing and updating, as some goals are achieved or abandoned. Bobbye and Britton have many of these sheets which they have saved over the years as testimony to the fact that they DID achieve them. They serve as a reminder that not only is growth possible, but it is one reason we have remained friends and lovers over the years.

Chapter 2

Growth: The Philosophy of Wedding versus Marriage

The potential for a thriving marital relationship begins with the wedding, but it takes time and a concerted effort for a couple to enjoy the full flower of satisfaction in the relationship called marriage. A large number of couples who divorce before their first anniversary proved that they don't have a culture that waits for the roots to develop. Many of these couples are robbing themselves of the very thing they hoped to achieve when they said, "I do."

Unfortunately, in today's society, people use "wedding" and "marriage" as synonymous terms. No wonder that the goal too often is to concentrate wholly on elaborate wedding plans rather than prepare for the marital relationship.

If the wedding is the desired goal, that goal is accomplished with an extraordinary amount of money and the blessings of friends and family. It is a beautiful time, certainly, and in some couples' minds it is the endpoint, an elaborate and special time of dresses, rituals, flowers, dinners, promises, and gifts.

From the standpoint of society, parents, bridal services, caterers, photographers, wedding coordinators, and many times the church as well, responsibility for couple assistance ends at this point. The couple has been assured that this is "their day" and they should make the most of it. Society will be pleased to welcome the new couple. The garden is planted and ready.

When the wedding is over, the bills are eventually paid, the last of the wedding attendants and the visiting family have departed, and the happy couple has left for the honeymoon, everyone involved can now relax, get back to their daily business, and consider their job "done." What happens to the couple after "their day" is largely up to them, in the minds of most of those who participated. Too many newlyweds have no instruction book about turning their wedding into a marriage of a lifetime, and they are yet to acquire the skills they will need in order to have a lasting marriage.

The Maces believed that all couples have the ability to affect their future together in a positive way. Some couples are better equipped than others, of course, depending on what has already happened to them, what helpful skills they learned in their families of origin, what resources they are willing to acquire, and how focused and realistic they are regarding what their goals are for their marriage.

The Maces' developing philosophy regarding marriage comes from their experiences of living and studying in various and diverse cultures. Part of their philosophy also comes from their own lives together as they, like all couples, sought to blend two personalities, backgrounds, ideas, and ambitions into a workable couple whole.

Here is the interview where they explain their unique concepts on growth as each couple, like pioneers, seeks to discover their own gifts and those of their partner, as well as a discovery and awareness of the ways those gifts can be used in the development of an abiding relationship:

> ***Bobbye:*** How would you define marriage? And why did the two of you want to study marriage customs in other countries?
>
> ***David:*** Let me take the second question first. I did my PhD. dissertation on Hebrew customs of marriage. Then I made a study

of the Latin legal structures as practiced in the Roman Empire. You could not make sense of how the early church formulated its doctrine of marriage, you see, without looking into its Semitic roots and into the beliefs and practices of the early church.

From these two pieces of research, I *decided that the center of my studies would be the family and that the center of the family was the couple*. Next, I went to the British Museum Reading Room where with all the spare time I could muster I read every book I could find in the English language on sex, marriage, and the family. I read a number of books in French, German, and Italian and many books in translation. By the end of my investigation, I knew the full range of the western world's accumulation of information about these subjects.

That was my starting point. And it gave me a clue that I could not be a well-informed specialist in marriage unless I saw it in the whole sweep of human culture. Travels to investigate other cultures would have to be off in the future, but I knew that is what I wanted to do.

Bobbye: You decided quite early then that marriage would be your specialty. Just so I have the timeline straight, when did this happen?

Vera: We were married in 1933 and David had already decided that this would be his field. Even when he was working for the Methodists in the London slums, this was what he wanted to do. It just took a while because of the demands of WWII to get the resources together to begin. And I knew when I first met David that I wanted to join in this exciting life-work.

I already had a master's degree in marriage and family. And I have always been interested in the historical position of women. For many years before I met David, I headed up a Women's Organization that had several associated counterparts in other countries. It was out of my work at this time that I developed a very broad worldview. It seemed to me that by studying other cultures, when the opportunity came, I could develop my personal status as an Internationalist.

David: Yes, on the day that we can apply for citizenship as an Internationalist, I will apply for it. I have always said so.

Britton: What does Internationalist mean?

David: Citizens of the world. "My country, right or wrong," just means little to us. We are proud of our English heritage, I don't want to underestimate that, but we are alive to the many great contributions that other countries have made to this world. We have made friends all around the world. I have said that if we were flying and had to parachute out of some airplane that was having mechanical problems, we would not have to go far to connect with someone we knew.

Vera: I want to say that I feel I am a patriot. But all the same, under the guise of patriotism, I think it's possible for many people to feel bigoted toward others. The world is a whole. I don't think you can say that just because you were born in one part of the world, none of the rest of it matters. My designation of myself as an Internationalist is all bound up with my love of history. Being an Internationalist does not reflect negatively on your patriotism.

David: Yes, when you have lived and worked with people of all cultures and found many of them to be beautiful people, it is hard to accept the idea that if they are not a citizen of your country, they are somehow an inferior person. You KNOW that is not true.

Bobbye: And in your travels and studies on all these different cultures, what did you find out about marriage?

David: We learned that there is a historical sequence of events taking place causing changes and transitions. It is not specifically confined to one culture. It is a worldwide movement, although those trends and transitions happen faster in the more westernized cultures.

We learned, for example, that the patriarchal family system is to be found in the majority of cultures. A matriarchal system is found only in relatively isolated communities and then, when you really examine it, it is matrilineal, not matriarchal.

We think in America that the Black community is matriarchal, like pockets of Africa and the Caribbean, but that is not strictly true. It was really the breaking down of the family system in the time of slavery that led to this assumption. The patriarchal system has been in place for several centuries, supported by all the great religions of the world. But everywhere the patriarchal system is in the process of breaking down, and a more democratic or egalitarian family system is being born.

We found that multi-linear marriages are being tried once again, as they were in the time of Julius Caesar. We found some polygamy still being practiced, although that was only in small areas of ruthless male dominance. We found the despotic rule of one family figure, still carried on as it was in earlier cultures which referred to it as a dynasty. And just like in those dynastic years. It still creates such enormous intrigues and plots by the extended family, that it is doomed to failure.

We found that many cultures still practice, with varying degrees of success, the so-called nuclear family, which some say has developed since the Industrial Revolution, but we say has been practiced for centuries. We know, for example, that in the fifth century in China, which was supposed to be the Golden Age of the extended family, only a small proportion of wealthy land-owners were able to keep the concept alive. The vast majority of the population, as you can see from the art, tapestries, and historical records of the time, practiced the nuclear family system (one mother, father, and children living in one household).

We found many new social experiments of the family as cultures move away from the traditional and try new forms and shapes of family configurations. Some of the new experiments are due to rising health costs; some come about as drug addictions, crime, and war injuries take their toll. But we all have to admit that changes in marriage and family are historical and always in flux.

> ***More and more we are seeing the companionship marriage as a trend, as couples around the world are striving together to achieve their full relational potential even as they work toward the success of their own personal goals and ideals.***

These couples are trying to be open and honest with each other on a daily basis. They are seeking to accept anger-disagreement as opportunities for growth. They are committed to the concept of shared power.

Unless you understand this point, you can say that marriage is dying out and collapsing. In fact, the new trends are showing an increasing respect for a quality couple life. *We are convinced that the patterns of the companionship marriage are essential for the world picture of learning to live together.*

Bobbye: Let's go back to my first question then. How do YOU define marriage?

David: I would define marriage as the achievement that a couple has when they embark together after a wedding. My way of defining marriage is not in terms of its precise legal status but in terms of

> *the quality of the relationship between the two people.*
> *A marriage happens when both partners are satisfied with that quality.*

It is very clear to me that a wedding is not a marriage. Marriages take time, and many couples simply do not wait long enough for any kind of quality relationship to develop.

Vera: But, David, the legalistic aspect of the union cannot be overlooked. If you apply for a passport, for example, you will have to check some box that labels you as Married, Divorced,

Single, Widowed, etc. You will fill out the same forms for taxes and applications of all kinds. It is your legal status. You can't just throw it out. You have been married according to the laws of the land. Aren't you overlooking that?

David: Of course, marriage is a legal concept. I am talking about a philosophical concept. And philosophically the terminology has got us confused. "Marriage" takes time for adjusting to change and growth. "Wedding" just starts you in that direction.

A wedding is an undertaking on the part of two people to set out on an adventure of trying to achieve a marriage. Unfortunately, throughout history, we have called a wedding a marriage and used the terms interchangeably. But I don't think we are justified in doing so.

The Swiss theologian Karl Barth once made a very interesting statement. He said that the Catholic Church has no doctrine of marriage. Since the Catholic Church considers marriage a sacrament, Barth was challenged on that statement. But he stuck to his guns. And he said that the church does not have a doctrine on marriage; it has a doctrine on weddings.

The wedding is when a couple enters into the state of matrimony with the blessing of the church. But what happens inside of the marriage is not the concern of the church. When the wedding is over, the responsibility of the church has ended for the quality of the relationship in the marriage. Therefore, said Barth, there is no doctrine of marriage.

That is the point I am trying to highlight, and it is a philosophical point but a valid one. It is time that society took seriously its responsibility for equipping brides and grooms to take the time and make the adjustments to produce a marriage of great quality and satisfaction. The responsibility does not stop when the wedding is over.

Britton: There is a current phenomenon called cohabitation. It has recently been widely studied and examined, at least by the news media. It seems to have become quite prevalent. How would that fit into your ideas on marriage for those who simply bypass the wedding and move in together, sometimes even parenting children together?

David: I can't give you an exact philosophical or theological line between who is "married" and who isn't, because it doesn't exist. I think that if the couple is working toward growth in their relationship, if they are raising a family together and are responsible in every way, I would say they are "married."

I know that the media refers to this state as "cohabitation," but I would call it instead of an unregistered marriage. Defining marriage as a *high quality of life for two people*, I think many of those couples deserve the title. I say this even though the statistics we have concerning break-ups for those co-habiting couples suggest they do not have a success rate even as good as those legally married.

And there is an interesting piece of side information about how cultures interact and influence each other. In Scandinavia, for example, a misunderstanding about an early church tradition regarding weddings led to a kind of sexual revolution worldwide. Scandinavia stood alone for over 1,000 years while Christianity swept over Europe. And when it finally came to their cultures, there was a misunderstanding of an Old Testament concept of—we call it engagement—what's the word for it?

Vera: Betrothal?

David: That's it, betrothal. The early church as it began to influence Scandinavia insisted that a couple come for a solemn ceremony of betrothal, along with family and friends. There was even an exchange of rings. Then after a prescribed period, the couple was to be married in the same church.

But what really happened was that after the solemn ceremony and exchange of vows, the couple just started living together. They felt there was no need for a second ceremony with all the further formality and expense. The betrothal ceremony was so formal, the church liturgies so strict, that the couple felt "married" from the moment that the ceremony was over.

Then as the betrothal ceremony fell away, couples simply moved in together. And that is how the loose standards of Scandinavian sexual behavior influenced the other European countries and eventually America.

If the early church had not made a great fuss about the betrothal ceremony and if the Scandinavian cultures had not misunderstood the concept, they might have followed the standards of other European cultures and just had a wedding. It's a fascinating piece of history about what eventually influenced the sexual revolution of the 1960s in the US.

Bobbye: Let's come back to the two of you and the beginnings of your relationship. How did it start?

David: It did not begin with romantic love. We developed a friendship first, connected to the fields in which both of us were working.

Vera: In fact, it began with a public argument. In your speech at a conference, you were taking issue with something I had said in a newsletter for the women's organization I worked for. I felt rebuffed.

David: Perhaps I was testing you.

Vera: How?

David: To see if you were the kind of person I could cooperate with. To see if we had compatible goals. I had been watching you for a while, but I did not want to have the kind of relationship with you that could not accept tensions and disagreements.

I would not want to spend my life with a person who got offended every time I said something that was not to her liking.

What I think happened to us was that we developed a friendship based on common goals and common concerns and to some extent common interests. What we found in each other was a person who interpreted life purposefully. That was important to both of us.

Vera: But we really saw each other very rarely in those years. You said that you had been watching me, but I didn't know about it. I think our real relationship depended on the pen. David bought some calendars one Christmas from some needy person, and he sent me a calendar as a present. I wrote him a letter thanking him. Then he wrote me a letter in reply, and I wrote back, and soon we were having lunch together.

David: Yes, and we began having lunch together regularly. I think we were making a friendship, discovering companionship.

Vera: You sent me the calendar at Christmastime, and we got engaged in June. And in those five months, you came several times to my lodging and we talked. Then in the spring, I remember, you came to a funeral and I met you there. When we talked after the funeral, that was the first time that I was aware that I was fond of you. It was the end of January when the correspondence first started; it was the end of June when we got engaged. And we were married thirteen months later.

Bobbye: So, you started your relationship as friends with kindred ideas and goals. When you got married, did you have any idea of the kind of marriage you wanted to have?

David: Very definitely. We saw our marriage as a sharing of our lives, in order that we might together benefit others. We thought that we could do more together than we could do separately. We even thought that our united actions would be more far-reaching than our separate actions.

Our friendship, our moving into love, and our eventual marriage were all closely linked. We had a feeling that we had a common destiny. We believed that we belonged together. And after our marriage not for one moment did we think we would not be a couple; even through the roughest patches, we simply knew that somehow, we had to work it through.

Growth as individuals and eventually growth as marriage partners was from the beginning a primary consideration. Both of us intended to do everything we could to grow our relationship and to stay close as friends and as lovers. It was a mutual goal and one we embraced from the beginning. We intended to make it work.

Britton: That is beautiful. Sounds like from the beginning you were intentional about staying in it for the long run. Do you feel that divorce is one alternative that a couple today should not consider in their relationship?

David: I think that would depend on their concept of marriage. Divorce was very difficult to get at the time we were married. But it would have been unthinkable for us because we thought we were called into this relationship. And that was it.

As long as we were both functioning, we were committed to each other, with no question about it whatsoever. If we had gone into marriage as one of the things you do in life, like taking a job or buying a house, then we would have said there were options. It's a matter of how you interpret marriage.

If marriage is just a decision you make, then the couple may give each other the freedom to break it off if it is not working out and hope it will be better the next time. From that standpoint, I would have no difficulty in understanding a decision to divorce.

For those who feel marriage is a calling, a life-long commitment, I would have difficulty in understanding a decision to divorce. It all depends on your definition of marriage.

Bobbye: Do you know the novel, *Jane Eyre*?

David: Of course.

Bobbye: Well, I taught that novel to sophomore girls in high school last spring. They had a hard time understanding why Rochester just didn't divorce Bertha when she developed a horrible mental illness and had to be chained up in order to protect others. Rochester was in love with Jane Eyre although legally married to Bertha. The sophomore girls thought that a simple way out of the difficulty was a divorce.

I tried to tell them that divorce was very rare in those days, and also that if Rochester had somehow managed to get a divorce, it would have put him under such a social stigma that he could not have married Jane anyway. But to young girls, today divorce is so much a part of their world that it is hard for them to imagine a time when that was not true. They had a hard time with all the suffering that Rochester and Jane went through when to them divorce seemed such an easy solution.

Vera: Yes, I remember a conversation I overheard on the top of a double-decker bus years and years ago in London. Two girls were talking about another girl who had just got engaged. This girl was Catholic and one of the girls on the bus said, "I wonder if she realizes that there goes the possibility of a divorce."

Britton: What about the old idea that a man's word is his bond? People in earlier times could even borrow money at a bank on the basis of the fact that they said they would pay it back. A handshake was supposedly all it took.

I once leased a house from a landlord just on my word that I wanted it and would come back to occupy it in a few weeks. The landlord saved it for me just on the basis of my word, even though she told us later that all her family and friends cautioned her about this. She was very relieved when we finally moved in and paid the first month's rent.

David: Yes, I belong to the old school which understands the importance of someone's "word" to his reputation. I would be very disappointed in myself if I failed to live up to a promise I made to someone. I am probably overly meticulous about it, but it is a concept I have of myself:

But this "word as bond" in marriage has another side to it. It suggests a certain rigidity and an inability to change. And part of the nature of marriage is dynamic; it demands change and adjustment. It calls for growth. Not to do it can be a kind of constricting or petrifying quality.

The openness and fluidity of modern life have released people from this restriction about changing their mind on anything. The flexibility of thought and readiness to change is important, inside and outside of marriage. But it has also invaded the idea of commitment.

I can be open to growth and change all my life. Education is one example of learning new ideas that modify convictions and opinions that we may have held earlier.

Bobbye: I think a real friend is one that will let you change your mind and won't hold you to a former opinion or idea just because you used to think something or other.

David: Yes, we have exalted some of the virtues of the past, even in marriage. Some people feel that you just have to stay the way you always have been. You cannot change. And in the marriage relationship, that makes it unnecessarily hard.

> ***Life brings change, and when we can be flexible and make changes with it, we grow as persons and as marriage partners.***

Bobbye: But what about the words of the marriage ceremony, "till death do us part," "for better or for worse," "as long as we both shall live"?

David: The marriage ceremonies that I have seen all involve a commitment to duty. There is no commitment to growth. What we are doing is to say to the bride and groom, "Look, you are making a solemn vow that however the marriage turns out, however miserable you are, you will stay with it."

I don't mind that, but what I do mind is holding people to a standard of duty without ever giving them any insights or information about how to achieve their goals and fulfill the dreams that both have. That should be the duty of the church, to equip brides and grooms at the time of the wedding.

Vera: In other words, you can decide whether it will be better or worse?

David: Yes, the condition of whether it will be better or worse is not some blind fate, some trick of circumstance, which leads you into misery, but you have to stay with it. You can make a choice about improving things, but you don't have the power to make that choice if you don't have the relational equipment to choose.

What I say is that a commitment to duty is all right as long as with it goes a commitment to growth. If you don't develop your marriage, and you don't work on your potential, it will be worse and not better. And you will have done it. When society does not equip those who are marrying with the relational skills and concepts they need to grow their marriage, it is an intolerable lack of understanding.

Britton: Have you ever written a marriage ceremony?

David: No, I haven't.

Britton: I have started asking the bride and groom to write things into the ceremony that they want to accomplish. There are certain words and ideas that I feel should remain in the marriage ceremony, but I have certain areas that I leave blank for them to establish their goals for their future, how they want to grow together.

David: That's good. But there's still another aspect of this. Why do we have a public wedding ceremony at all if the bride and groom are only making a commitment to each other? They could do that privately and save lots of money.

Isn't the family, their friends, their relatives, even the church if that is where they are having their ceremony, making a public commitment to them as well that they will help them grow their marriage?

We all need to take marriage more seriously from the standpoint that the couple needs to have family and friends who will stand with them through the "better or worse" and help them in their difficult times.

It almost seems today that all the church does is just provide the building. The wedding is not a part of the church ministries themselves, and no one attending the wedding commits themselves to teach and instruct and share in the lives of those who are getting married. At least, someone should promise to stand with them for their first year together as they move from "wedding" to "marriage."

Vera: I want to ask you something, Britton. I know that you are a Single Adult Minister. Is it the assumption that the divorced people in your single's group want to marry again?

Britton: I would say the vast majority of them want to marry again, even those who have come out of a bad situation.

Vera: That's interesting because it indicates that they are not against marriage.

David: Yes, and that fits the latest national statistics, where three out of five of all women marry again after divorce, and four out of five of all men.

Vera: What about those who have never married?

Britton: Many of them hope to be married someday. But I tell them not to expect it. I say, "Assume you will never get married. Then if it does happen, it can be a surprise rather than a disappointment." "Just get on with your life," I tell them. "This is the only chance you have to live."

David: That's good. They should be developing their own resources, and if they do get married someday, which will be helpful in the new relationship. Personal growth is the precursor of couple growth, and even if the person never becomes part of a couple, there is a full, rich life available. What one does in the present often determines how one will handle things in the future.

The pressures to get married at an early age are almost always dooming the couple to failure. The greatest chance for marital success for a woman is between the ages of twenty-five and twenty-seven. The greatest chance for marital success for a man is between the ages of twenty-seven and thirty-one. That gives both of them the chance:

- to be on their own for a while,
- to establish themselves as single adults,
- to learn skills in a dating relationship,
- to fulfill some of their personal goals for growth and accomplishment.

Also, there are some couples who feel that after the wedding it is as though they were put in a room by themselves and someone else turned a key in the lock. When this happens—and it does happen with disappointing regularity—it suggests all the cultural catch-words about marriage, such as "the ball and chain" or "they got hitched." For these couples, there is little in the way of joyful anticipation of what they can expect from the marriage relationship. They feel a constriction that makes growth impossible.

Britton: For a couple going into a second marriage after a divorce, are there certain things that they should come to grips with?

David: I would say that unless the person who has divorced has worked through the meaning of that failure and squarely faced what happened and what it means, the chances are that they will fail again. What I have found rather strikingly is that people who say that it was the other person's fault that the marriage failed are the people who are likely to fail again.

To accept responsibility for the failure of the marriage is a healthy thing. To be open to the idea that you have to be flexible to change and growth the next time around puts you in a good spot. There is seldom such a thing as an innocent partner and a guilty partner. Both are responsible, perhaps not equally, but both are responsible. By accepting your share of the responsibility, you are preparing yourself in the best possible way for the next time around.

Britton: I think many persons entering marriage the second time around are very fearful. They are scared to think that they might fail again. Do you think this is a good or a bad trait?

David: I think I would prefer being fearful of being overconfident. But like all fears, this fear may paralyze their capacity to do their best. Or it could serve as an incentive to do their best. Fear is a two-edged sword.

A person must work through the responsibility for what happened in the first marriage. If that person has taken adequate time for this to happen and has not been stampeded into a second marriage trying to escape the judgment of the failure of the first one, that person will probably find the happiness they were hoping for.

It's important not to be rushed into a second marriage. The statistics are showing us that this is not very promising. Second marriages have an even higher rate of failure than first ones, second only to teenage marriages, and I think it comes about largely because someone rushes the development of the relationship. Personal growth takes time and cannot be rushed. Couple growth takes time, as well.

> ***Growth is the great thing that keeps a marriage alive and interesting. It should be the goal from the time of the wedding.***

If we can somehow find a way to convince society of this fact, many divorces will be prevented and the decay and boredom that marks other marriage relationships today will be changed.

The Woods' Experience with the Philosophy of Wedding Versus Marriage

From the time of the wedding, the Mutual Commitment to Growth offers the possibility for change and growth for both partners. When a couple goes through the "door" of commitment, each of them often sees new choices of behavior and develops better ideas of how growth might work in their unique relationship.

It might also mean that each partner is more alert to opportunities to correct old habits that are not helpful for a growing relationship. Making assumptions and failing to check for their accuracy is one old habit that Bobbye identified early in their marriage. As an only child, she was used to processing experiences and interpretations in her head, without the necessity of sharing them with anyone else. It was a habit that was hard to change and one that for a long time seemed unnecessary to change.

But shortly after the Woods were trained in Marriage Enrichment, Bobbye came home from the grocery store with several heavy paper sacks. When the garage door opened, she saw Britton's car and knew he was home. In addition, the garage door opener had made loud noises, so she assumed that he knew she was home from the grocery store. She heard the sounds from the living room that said he was watching the TV news, but she assumed that he knew she would struggle with the heavy grocery sacks and that he would come to help her. She assumed that is what all loving partners would do.

He did not come. She rattled drawers, banged doors, and loudly slammed down a grocery sack in the kitchen as a hint that he should come and help. He still did not come. Then she assumed that Britton did not "know" she needed help because he did not want to "know."

Just before she really got angry about all the information and assumptions she was processing in her mind, she remembered their Mutual Commitment to Growth. "Whose concern is this?" she asked herself. She had to admit that it was hers and that there was a possibility that he did not even hear that she had arrived at home.

She went to the stairs to the living room and asked if he would help with the grocery sacks. He immediately got up and helped.

Making assumptions about the partner's motivation and devising actions from those assumptions can be a slippery slope to falling down into an angry scene. Expecting the partner just to "know" what we want and need is unrealistic. Assuming we know what is in any person's mind is also unrealistic.

With an agreement concerning the Commitment to Growth, we can easily check our assumptions for accuracy and avoid those common scenes caused by old habits of assumption.

Couple Exercise

Discuss some of the benefits to a couple of making a mutual commitment to growth. Then take turns answering the following questions.

1. Of the goals you listed as part of your Growth Plan, what is the one that you most want to accomplish?
2. What is one impediment to accomplishing that goal?
3. What is one thing you could do to make that goal happen?
4. What is one way your partner could help you with that accomplishment?

Chapter 3
Couple Growth

After many years of pursuing their life goals of helping marriages succeed, the Maces realized their own relationship needed more of the growth they had been recommending to other couples all around the world. Fortunately, they knew how to get it, and here is a record of the process they used to re-establish intimacy and couple connection. It is heartening and encouraging today to see that at any point in the couple's life journey, new insights and enjoyment can happen:

> ***David:*** At one point toward the middle of our lives together, we began to take stock of what we had accomplished and what we had yet to do. I began to read back through all the columns I had written for the magazines and all the early books on marriage we had published, and we discussed all our work as we reviewed it for each other. And we came to the conclusion that there had been three stages in our development as we saw not only what we wanted to do for other people's marriages but also our own.
>
> The first stage of our work, we discovered, was when we got the Marriage Guidance Center going in London. That was

our big accomplishment just after the ending of WWII. Our emphasis was on saving the marriages that were coming apart largely from the many pressures of the war years and helping them in the midst of social chaos. At that time, we regarded our marriage as secure. We were safe. We were on the land, you see, and they were struggling in the water.

Vera: Compassion motivated us to do something for them, to throw out a lifeline.

David: From the London Marriage Guidance Council, I founded several branches in other countries and for a while I directed all their services. Then I became head of the International Union of Marriage Counselors, an organization that had members from around the world, many of whom were trying to help couples devastated by problems which before the war had been largely undiscovered.

I became a consultant for the United Nations and UNESCO, and every year Vera and I would go to other countries to work in the Marriage Guidance Councils. And it was all part of the same mission, you see, going out to help others. Counseling was the medium. That was where we started. That was what we knew.

Vera: Rescue was the goal, I think, as we tried to respond to the many needs we saw both in our own country and in others.

David: The second stage for us in the development of our life's work was maintenance and education. It came when we saw that if people never fell into the water, they wouldn't need to be rescued. The emphasis became giving out information. The emphasis was on maintaining marital health. Keep a sound footing and you won't fall into the water.

We were not so much trying to save the people as to inform them about how to take care of themselves and thus avoid any potential disasters in a relationship. The writing that I did for magazines and newspapers was full of advice for couples. This was true in England and then again as we moved the family to the US. *The Woman's Home Companion* even called the column "Can This Marriage Be Saved?" All our speaking and writing was geared to maintenance and education.

Vera: Yes, we were putting up symbolic guardrails to protect marriages.

David: Of course, we know now that it was not very effective. We wrote books and gave lectures and appeared on all kinds of radio and television shows, which was almost useless.

Vera: I think you are exaggerating here.

David: Perhaps, but only for emphasis. But in the midst of disseminating education for the purpose of maintenance, *we discovered that our own marriage needed maintenance.*

Vera: All marriages need maintenance.

Britton: Even yours?

David: Yes, indeed. And at this point, we became aware of the need to work on our own marriage to keep it healthy. Simple maintenance was not enough, we soon discovered. We wanted something more. We wanted something that we had not yet experienced.

Vera: We saw that "growth" was a word that we needed to apply to ourselves. We took it very seriously. We had started out absolutely committed to the idea of growth, but somehow, we had busied ourselves with other important things and had left that commitment to fending for itself.

Britton: You had been busy for years as a couple devoted to helping others, and you came to a place where you saw the importance of applying those ideas to your own relationship.

David: Yes, but it was not really a new idea. We had first used it with the Quakers as early as 1969 to explain the primary concept of the new movement that would later become Marriage Enrichment. Here's how it came about, as I remember.

The Quakers had received a grant that paid us to train Quaker couples in how to do couple dialogue. They brought in couples from all over the US to a meeting in Philadelphia. Then the couples went home and started groups in their cities. After six months, we all returned for a second meeting. They reported what had been happening in the groups they had become a part of, and we reported what had been happening in the groups we continued to train.

We all talked about the exciting new ideas we were involved in, but we referred to them as "couple development." We lacked a word to describe what was happening to these couples. Finally, we seized on the word "growth" with a good bit of eagerness, and by the time the meeting was concluded, we all saw that word would be the primary concept of the new movement. We even used the word "enrichment," also, as I remember.

Vera: So that's how we got from the first stage to the third. David and I saw clearly what was happening in the lives of other couples, and we saw how we had neglected it in our own relationship. We decided to correct that neglect right away by establishing a new growth plan. No longer was mere maintenance going to be enough for us.

David: Yes, and that's important. The average couple thinks of their marriage as something that must be maintained, just as a house has to be maintained. There are certain duties that must be fulfilled, and at some time they have to meet some obligations in order that the marriage may go on. But the average couple does not think in terms of personal expansion and personal growth. They certainly do not think in terms of couple growth.

I think that many of the couples who come to Marriage Enrichment are from the maintenance class. They feel a certain responsibility for their marriage. They feel a responsibility to the family. They know that marriage and family are important to both personally and to the society in general, but under the pressures of work and making a living, many husbands and wives have done little but maintain both marriage and family. I think we might have fallen into that category.

Vera: But there are those couples who come to Marriage Enrichment from the counseling area, who have been hurt or wounded by troubles in their own relationship.

David: Yes, of course, but those couples will soon see that they need counseling or remediation of some kind. Typically, couples think of their marriage as an important, just as we did, an investment that must be maintained and taken care of. They just don't know how to go about its maintenance as efficiently as they would like. They have never yet considered the idea of growth.

Bobbye: I have not read it, but I know that one of your books is called *How to Have a Happy Marriage*. It sounds like you could have substituted the word "growing" instead.

Vera: That's what we wanted to call it. But the publishers thought "happy" would be catchier and insisted on that change.

Bobbye: What would be some ways a couple could experience growth?

David: We think it all starts with their awareness of its importance. Once there is a real discovery of what commitment to growth might mean to the relationship, any couple can easily work out what they really want. The concept of growth opens up new vistas both of themselves as partners and of the relationship itself. That is the point where we once started, and that is the point we came back to when we decided we wanted a fuller relationship.

Here's how we see it: *the commitment to growth provides the motivation, the gas, the fuel to take you down the road.*

The communication system allows you to know and show who you are, and it also allows you to receive the same information about the partner. It also shows where you are in your relationship. *It locates you in your world.*

Britton: It's your roadmap?

David: Yes.

Bobbye: You said that the communication system allows you to know who you are. What does that mean?

David: Basically, the starting point for an effective communication system is an awareness of your own feelings, a recognition of what's going on inside yourself. Most people displace a lot of their feelings or evade them or feel guilty about them. But you have to be self-aware and acknowledge what you are feeling. That is important information that you must communicate to your partner. If you don't know what your feelings are, you cannot even begin to share who you are, and intimacy with the partner will be very limited.

> ***Once you are committed to growth, it is essential to let the partner know where you are and what you want.***

We are not really trained for intimacy in our society. We see little children saying what they really think and feel, and we say, "Oh, how sweet and innocent." But inside we are thinking that they had better grow out of it fast or they will be in for some bitter experiences. And that is partially true. We need to be prudent about what we say to others. We need to have some defenses for interaction with others on a daily basis. That is only smart and a way of taking care of ourselves in the world.

But at the same time closing ourselves off from others gives us no preparation for what we will need in a quality relationship. There we will need to take down those defenses that can be helpful in daily society. There we will need to share ourselves. That is hard to do, but it is the only way to become intimate with someone.

If two people try to live in a close relationship and withhold themselves and their deepest feelings, it's impossible to have the very intimacy that makes growth and discovery a joy. So, the effective communication system begins with an awareness of yourself—who you are—and a willingness and ability to share that self with a loved and trusted companion.

Then the third part of the Primary Coping System is important too. *The capacity to make creative use of conflict gives you the ability to make continuing growth, both as individuals and as a couple.* Your conflicts locate your growth points. Resolving those conflicts releases you from past resentments and frustrations. Resolving the conflicts opens up the prospect of a great future together.

But it all starts with the commitment to growth. And that commitment can happen at any age or any stage of the relationship.

The Woods' Experience with Couple Growth

Like random acts of kindness, loving behaviors are always welcome in close relationships. In addition, loving behaviors show the commitment to growth, keep that commitment on both partners' minds, and help create an environment for more intimacy. Sometimes for variety and fun, the loving behaviors might be a surprise.

Perhaps leaving post-it notes for each other could be that surprise. Bobbye and Britton leave lyrics to love songs in unusual places for the other to find. Bobbye came to the kitchen one morning, and as she turned on the light in the pantry, there was a post-it note that told her, "You light up my life."

Notes have appeared as bookmarks, on toothbrushes, in underwear drawers, and in other unexpected places. Bobbye changed the words to a song she heard at exercise class one morning and put them on a post-it note on Britton's pillow. The song said, "Brave and strong/So smart and studly, too/All night long/I get to sleep with you/Ba—by."

Funny, sexy, or romantic e-mails or texts work as well, just to keep both partners aware that new growth as a couple is welcome and wanted. Loving behaviors like the post-it notes, texts, or e-mails are fun to create, fun to anticipate, fun to do, fun to receive, and fun to recall.

Couple Exercise

1. What one action could our relationship take that could best help with our couple growth?
2. What are three words that would describe our relationship today?
3. What loving behavior do you especially appreciate from your partner?

Chapter 4

Growth and Change

In 1988, the first International Marriage Enrichment Conference (IMEC) was held in Atlanta, Georgia. The Maces brought together professionals who were already making outstanding contributions to the brand-new market of couples who wanted to learn skills that would help them grow in their marital relationship.

Even though in the past the targeted market for providing social change had been the fragile couples who were in trouble and in dire need of counseling and rehabilitation, now the field was changing directions. The new emphasis reflected innovative programs that were positive and preventive. The new market would be to healthy couples:

- who had already discovered how to avoid serious problems,
- who wanted to grow closer throughout their lifetime by assimilating new practical skills,
- who were determined to affect the families of the future by modeling those new and practical skills.

It was an exciting time, with new energy, new perspectives, and new directions.

Along with the hopeful couples in attendance at the international event, the audience was made up of the various Boards, Agencies, and

Universities who had sent representatives to learn about the new ideas of addressing the issues that could best help relationships to prosper. Even the US Navy Family Support Program had sent Bill Coffin to learn additional methods of aiding military couples and families. These representatives were eager to hear what new materials, programs, and philosophies these pioneers and professionals might offer.

Father Gabriel Calvo was there from Spain (originator of Marriage Encounter), as were Phyllis and Sherod Miller of the Couple Communication Program; David Olson, designer of the marital inventory called Prepare and Enrich; Bernard Guerney, Jr. of Relationship Enhancement; Lori Heyman Gordon, who founded PAIRS; Leon and Antoinette Smith, fellow pioneers who designed and worked with programs for marriages in the United Methodist Church.

The Maces presented one of their ideas, a novel concept which they called the *Mutual Commitment to Growth*. This commitment, they said, opens the "door" for all interested couples to begin a consideration of their marital adventure in a new way.

Such a commitment asked them to regard everything that happens to them—even their disagreements—as an opportunity to learn more about each other. The Mutual Commitment to Growth anchored the couple and asked them to create a custom-made marriage which allowed each individual to grow as a person but also featured the growth of the relationship itself.

Couples were no longer committed *JUST* to stay together. Instead, they were being asked:

- to commit to the radical new idea of the growth of their relationship,
- to explore ways of moving their union to a new level of understanding and support,
- to give to both persons involved a way to consider, articulate, and achieve their own goals and dreams and to also consider mutual goals for the relationship, even if the points of view differ toward those goals.

One partner may see snow as beautiful, for example, and the other may see it as a chore falling from the sky. But both points of view are important when you are trying to define, redirect, and achieve a couple growth. Both persons need to respect and to understand the other's needs and ideas as they move together to a new level. Not all couple goals can be achieved, and it is important that both understand the reasons why some cannot.

The Mutual Commitment to Growth turns out to be a simple and effective philosophy toward elevating the relationship. It is an early emphasis on what educators today call the "us," that intangible entity between partners that is not the "you" nor the "me," but it is the couple relationship itself. The Maces were introducing a concept for strengthening that connection.

It was an early invitation to "manage" their relationship (a term later used effectively by Dr. John Van Epp), to take charge of it and custom-make it to the mutual satisfaction of both people involved. No longer was mere chance and circumstance the manager; the couple would become the manager, supported and aided by simple "tools" and skills which each could use.

The Mutual Commitment to Growth would be the "door," the flexible contract that changes as couples themselves change over the course of their lives. It could last a lifetime and equip couples for quality relationships.

Here is what the Maces said about two kinds of couple growth and the benefits of going through that "door" of commitment:

> ***David:*** There are two important kinds of couple growth that happen to most couples as they embark on the adventure of marriage. One is called *assimilation*. This is like a seed drawing in from its environment all the necessary ingredients to nourish the future plant.

Nothing grows in a vacuum; like plants, a couple is continually taking in from its daily environment. Paying attention to relevant information about marriage allows them to choose new ideas and interpretations to expand their daily awareness of what is happening to them.

Britton: Sometimes society says, "Get into a vacuum. Protect yourselves from a hostile world." But if couples do, they cut themselves off from seeing any models of couples who are experimenting with new skills of relating, trying new ideas, and taking in from their environment new information about healthy relationships.

David: Yes. Some couples get married, their friends wish them well—

Vera: It's the happily-ever-after wish.

David: Yes, and they go into a symbolic box and never see what other couples are thinking, doing, and experiencing. The very thing they need—*an environment that shows models of other couples dealing with issues and finding ways to balance work, family, and couple growth*—they withdraw from.

A couple can only have change and growth if they are motivated to change and grow, and the motivation quite often comes from seeing others do it. Modeling is a great stimulation toward change, and if a couple does not have modeling, as long as they have no way to see other marriages working on relevant issues, their motivation is very, very limited.

What often happens in the groups that we work with is that a couple identifies with a struggling couple and shares some of their own struggles, including couple dialogues about how they overcame those struggles and difficulties.

This quite often awakens in the first couple some long-forgotten dream about what they had hoped for, what they had really wanted in marriage but had given up on. But re-awakening the dream and REVIVING HOPE IS WHAT WE ARE REALLY DOING.

We are saved by hope. Without hope, we have no expectations; we have no motivation. If we are committed to the marriage from the standpoint of duty, we just stay where we are and accept whatever happens. We never consider change and never think about growth. If the relationship gets painful enough, we separate.

Bobbye: It sounds like couples have to be aware of what the environmental influences are. Assimilative growth seems to be a combination of couple-awareness and the willingness to hear what others are saying about marriage. Like the seed you talked about, the couple also needs to take in the nutrients for their specific relationship.

I think I may have a good example of assimilative growth. The first time I heard you two speak at a conference, I was alarmed that Vera sometimes interrupted while the two of you were speaking onstage. Since the two of you speak together about marriage, I realized that the interruptions often added something important to the point being made. But it was difficult for me to watch from the audience. I had never seen anyone do that. I thought it was not polite socially.

But David did not seem to mind; in fact, the two of you seemed quite comfortable with it. By the end of the evening, I was accepting it, although with a few reservations. I did refer to you after that evening, Vera, as "that woman who interrupted her husband on stage."

As I heard you two speak again at another conference, I noticed that interruptions were merely a conversational pattern for the two of you. Neither of you seemed to mind at all. In fact, this time I noticed that David interrupted you just as often as you did to him.

David: Yes, I have been reprimanded by feminist's for my interruptions on more than one occasion.

Bobbye: As I heard you speak together from the stage more often, I quit regarding it as a novelty and instead just listened to two people sharing their ideas with passion and good humor. Over time, in fact, I came to enjoy it. It shows Vera as an assertive woman who has things to say on her own and doesn't mind inserting them when she wants to. David does the same. It is a style that fits the two of you.

It took me a while, but I have assimilated the style with appreciation. I took it in from the environment of a couple speaking together to an audience. I sifted, tested, weighed, and measured it. And when that was done, I have found that it has made me want to know you both better.

And to go one step farther, now Britton and I even do the same thing when we speak to groups. That is real assimilation.

Is there another kind of couple growth?

David: There is also *adaptational growth*. I believe that in adaptational growth, conflict is the vital element because, without conflict, adaptational growth would not take place. It is only as two people interact and collide that adaptational growth happens.

It is a collision of wishes. That is a simple definition of conflict, but it hits the nail on the head. Without a collision of wishes, the couple would not be alerted to where they need to work. The positive value of conflict is demonstrated here. It's like a squishy noise in your car that says something needs to be fixed to help it run smoothly.

Britton: It's the squeaky wheel that gets the oil kind of thing?

David: Exactly. The Mutual Commitment to Growth is the "door," the contract, that gets things started, you see. It puts you on the alert for what you need from your environment. But assimilative growth and change may happen so slowly that the couple themselves do not see it right away. Adaptational growth, on the other hand, is sudden; it is the response to a clash or a calamity. It forces the person to face the fact that something needs to be done.

Bobbye: If you are saying that conflict or collision—and sometimes calamity—can lead to adaptational growth, aren't there people who feel that conflicts need to be avoided? And that a harmonious relationship only exists when there isn't conflict? That conflict only leads to trouble?

David: That's the tragedy. There are those who identify conflict as the Serpent in the Garden of Eden. And if the culture tells people that conflict is bad, they will run away from it. The couple has a clash of wishes, it escalates into a conflict, and they run away from it.

This gets repeated until they cannot take it anymore and either stoically resign themselves to ignore it or divorce. That is the tragedy. At the very point where the couple needs to get to work and listen to each other, they run away.

Britton: Many young couples in their first year of marriage are asked, "How are things going?" And they say (as they are expected to say), "FANtastic." They are really thinking, "If you only knew," but they do not know anything else to say to a society that is ambivalent about the potential value of conflict.

Vera: That's the "intermarital taboo."

David: Yes, the *intermarital taboo* is "I won't tell you what is going on in my marriage, and you don't tell me what is going on in yours." Then the couple splits up and society says, "What's the matter with John and Mary? I didn't know anything was wrong. They never said a thing."

Then because conflict is not seen as healthy or good, the couple does not seek any help to address what is going on until it reaches the level of the intolerable. Intervention sometimes helps—counseling or therapy—but they may have waited until both have little confidence in the relationship and little left to build on.

Then the couple often interprets the conflict publicly as "We are just not suited to each other." There is a deep error there, that idea of compatibility. I am happy to say that society, in general, has shifted away from this idea of mate selection and compatibility. The old idea was to find the right partner. If they were right for each other, all the contours of personality would fit and then—happily-ever-after.

Now that is all gone. Now we realize that adaptation means change. You have to MAKE the fit, not FIND it.

Adaptational growth faces the conflict, seeks to understand it, and uses it for the growth of the couple. In many ways, it is easier than assimilative growth because its visibility is quickly apparent.

Vera: I want to go back to what we were saying about conflict and calamity. I want to tell about a time when a calamity—a difficult separation—actually led to growth.

One of the most important periods in our marriage was a period of separation. We were separated totally for three years by WWII. After the fall of France, it looked very likely that England would be invaded. Our two daughters were invited to come to the US to stay in safety with family friends. They were too small to come alone, so I brought them. This was before Pearl Harbor, so America was not yet in the struggle. It was 1940, and a very bleak period of world history.

David stayed in London as an air raid warden. I had planned to go back immediately after the girls were settled in, but in December, after the US entered the war, ordinary citizens were not allowed to cross the Atlantic. So, I stayed here, separated from David to wait out the war. We wrote letters to each other, but it was not until 1943 that it was safe for me to return.

It took six weeks for a letter to come across the Atlantic, and then they were heavily censored. But during that three-year separation, our relationship grew. We did not feel the results of the growth until we all came back together as a family in 1945. But the growth was going on during the separation. Where does all that fit into this conversation on growth?

David: We did write letters, even if they were censored. And the thing that Marriage Encounter later established was that couples who cannot reach each other verbally can write down the things they most want to say and share them in that way. And we did that. We were able to pour out our hearts to each other in our letters in a way that we probably at that time could not have done even had we been together.

I particularly could not have done that; expressing my emotions was too hard. Somehow in letters, it was possible to do so. In fact, we were communicating very deeply through our letters. That communication allowed us to face the world conflict, to do the thing that kept us close throughout it, and to adapt as a couple.

And we came back together again with an enormous appreciation of being together. The war was a unique conflict or calamity, but because we used ways to stay close to each other during it, we found growth as a couple on the other side of it. It was an example of adapting to what was happening and using it to our advantage. When couples can adapt to their changing life circumstances, when they can talk to each other about what is happening to them and what is happening IN them, they can also use those circumstances for growth.

Change is the nature of life, yet too many couples during the busyness of life take the path of least resistance and let their relationship drift into staleness and distance.

Assimilative growth happens when a couple pays attention to their needs and helps each other draw in from their environment that will meet those needs. Adaptational growth happens when a couple addresses what they see going wrong between them—and in some cases around them—and seeks a way to resolve it.

On the same afternoon of interviews where the Maces explained two kinds of couple growth to us, they also added some additional insights into what brings about growth and what benefits a couple can expect:

> ***Bobbye:*** What needs to happen when a couple makes a contract together of a mutual commitment to growth? In other words, even though it will be different for each couple, say something about what the couple is going to get out of making that commitment?
>
> ***David:*** I think some of the common benefits will be a *combination of openness and closeness.* As couples get to the place that they can be open with each other, they will also perceive a new closeness, an intimacy that draws them into a circle-for-two that speaks volumes to their family and friends. When there is that special closeness, there comes also a desire to keep it by continuing to be open with each other.
>
> ***Vera:*** But why do we want to be intimate with a particular person? I believe we have a need as human beings to be intimate with someone, to touch and be touched by that person. Why did I want to be intimate with you?
>
> ***David:*** I think it's a question of establishing identity. Some people feel that identity is only established by standing on your own two feet and doing all life's tasks alone.
>
> Our definition of identity is *TO BE FULLY KNOWN AND DEEPLY LOVED.* If you are deeply loved, in spite of the fact that you are fully known, you know you are ok. You can function confidently in society, on the job, in the extended family, because you have had it confirmed that you are a competent and independent person capable of all manner of wonderful achievements.

It is within the couple that this identity is developed. The Mutual Commitment to Growth contract simply assures both that no one is going to walk away as they take the steps of self-disclosure that allows them to really know each other.

The child at first belongs to the parents in an authoritarian way, and one early duty is that he or she must break free and establish his or her own identity. This in psychology is called differentiation. It is a necessary step. But not until the child can begin to establish relationships on his own, he can begin to claim his deeper identity. The marriage relationship is the most important place for this to happen, and when it does, it is incredibly important.

When you know who you are, you begin to open yourself up to others. And this, in turn, deepens our concept of who we are. Those who keep themselves closed up, fearing that people would not like them if those people knew them fully, never get to the point of sustained intimacy with anyone at any time.

Britton: Once a lady came to my office and said, "I'm afraid that if I tell you what I'm about to tell you, you won't like me." That sounds like an example of her fear to be fully known.

David: But it also sounds like she was ready to take the risk because her need was so great.

Britton: I stopped to assure her that our relationship was not based on whatever she was going to tell me. I said that our friendship was deeper than that, and she relaxed and told me.

David: And yet the poet Rilke says that within each of us there is a private citadel that we can never let another person into; we do not even know ourselves well enough to understand what is inside that citadel.

Marriage is a special relationship where each appoints the partner as guardians of that solitude—that citadel—and what a celebration it is when each can allow a distance between them at the same time as they freely grow close to each other. It is a knowing each other intimately, while acknowledging there is a space unknowable in each of us. It is a couple's identity that is irreplaceable. Without a contract for commitment, no one is ever going to face fully the mystery of our own personalities, much less the mystery of another.

Bobbye: It sounds like Kahlil Gibran, who said that "the winds of heaven can dance between" a couple who give to each other freely but also remain independent of each other. In fact, I think that the poet also said that one tree could not grow in the shade of another tree. I hear that quoted at weddings sometimes.

Is there another part to experiencing couple growth?

David: Yes, in addition to the shared disclosure that leads to identity, there is the completing of communication cycles.

Bobbye: You'll have to explain that one.

David: It's the shared meaning, as they say in the Couple Communication program. I tell you what I think, then you tell me what you think I said as a way of sharing that meaning together. Then I either confirm or correct.

Vera: You can say, "You got it" or "No, that's not what I meant at all. Let me try that again."

David: It's a remedy for possible misunderstandings. And in the intimacy provided by self-disclosure and the growth that happens because of it, it is imperative that we understand each other. You cannot misunderstand me if we complete the cycle and you tell me back what you heard me say. Airplane pilots must do it. There it is a matter of life or death. It is a basic concept in important communication.

If I am going to tell you intimate personal things, I need to know that you understand me. I could ask you if you understand, and you might even say yes. But I would not really know if you do understand what I am telling you until I hear you say it back to me in your own words. That completes the communication. That is shared meaning.

That lets me know that you have heard the words that I needed to tell you about me. You don't have to agree with what I tell you, but completing the cycle helps me to know that we have now shared this information.

Britton: I can see how this would be an important aid to growth. Is there anything else that a couple can do to help gain the benefits of the Mutual Commitment to Growth?

David: *Affirmation* may be the most important factor in building the kind of intimacy that comes from this contract. All the studies in what makes strong marriages mention this one as essential to our sense of well-being. Praising each other, complimenting each other, expressing affection to each other—these are ways of growing and staying close to each other. In practicing the habit of daily positive interaction, we are becoming secure with each other and more confidently able to handle all the daily troubling trials that beset us.

This was a difficult concept for me to learn—to verbalize loving, positive words to those I love. You see, I grew up in Scotland among the most tight-lipped people in the world.

Britton: Oh, that's where they are? I was wondering where they lived.

David: Yes, Scotland is definitely the place. Changing my natural inclination to say nothing that was remotely personal to anybody has been a great change for me—a needed one certainly but a difficult thing to achieve. It is one of those accomplishments I am proudest of.

Vera: I learned about this Scottish reticence when I was barely a teenager and working as a nurse's aide after World War I.

There was a Scotsman in my ward who could neither read nor write. I found this very strange since he was obviously intelligent. Anyway, one of my duties was to write letters to his father. He had a hard time choosing anything to say, but he finally settled on telling about the food in the hospital. Then he said he was through; that was all he needed to say. I wrote down all the menus he could remember, and then I suggested that he might close "with love" or "from your affectionate son."

He looked deeply shocked. Then he said to me, "You should know better than that." "What are you talking about?" I asked. He told me that the right thing to say in closing the letter was "from your respectful son." "You should not use 'affectionate' or any words like that, not with MY father. He wouldn't like it."

David: Yes, that's exactly how it was when I was growing up in Scotland. In fact, there's an old story of a couple who have been married for fifty years. They were visiting friends, and the man asked the husband if they could step outside for a moment because there was one question he wanted to ask. He indicated that it was a hard and embarrassing question, but he said he needed to ask it.

"Now," he asked the husband, "after all these fifty years of living together, can you really say you love this woman?" "Oh," said the husband, "that's not a hard thing at all. Yes, I really love her, and I always have. In fact, sometimes it's all I can do not to tell her so."

That just epitomizes the whole situation. It was the environment I came out of. And that's pretty much the way it still is in Scotland. It's a great tribute to Vera that I learned to express my feelings to her and make her happy.

Bobbye: That's really sad, especially for young men growing up in that culture. Of course, they had feelings, but it sounds like there was no acceptable social way to express them.
It sounds like the culture deprives them of a part of their personalities—their emotions—and even makes them feel that there is something wrong with expressing tender feelings.

David: Yes, but that's what I came out of, and I've come a long way. I have really grown there, haven't I, dear?

Vera: Definitely.

Britton: How have you done that? Why did you make those changes?

David: Because I wanted my marriage to be successful, and I progressively came to see that I had to do this. Then I discovered that it was so rewarding, that now I like to have my relationships warm with everybody.

Vera: Did you ever feel that our marriage was threatened because you couldn't be warm and tender?

David: No, not threatened. But I did feel that I was not contributing to the quality of the relationship. And you were. I was way behind, and I wanted to catch up.

Bobbye: How did you become able to share your private feelings? Was it because you trusted Vera?

David: Yes. Trust certainly helped me to be able to bring out my positive feelings. But I also saw that bringing them out to Vera in the safety of our relationship was something good for me.

Britton: Vera, how were you able to help him?

Vera: I had never felt the same restrictions that he did. I grew up in Yorkshire, in England, and it was very different from Scotland. Then also it was a question of temperament. I just never had the difficulty that David did. And I grew up in a very different family from David.

When I was growing up, my father was both father and mother to me, not because my mother wasn't present but because she was deaf, and this cuts her off from many family interactions. But, fortunately, my father was very progressively "there." So, expressing my feelings to a man, and hearing feelings expressed to me, was a natural occurrence. In fact, it was something I wanted in a husband.

David: He was a very warm, friendly, and outgoing father.

Britton: How did you see David, since it sounds like at first, he was very different from your father? You were married when David wasn't so warm. What did you think?

Vera: I admired David's intellect and his capacity for ideas. I still do. It was very stimulating to hear his philosophies, but I think I just took the rest on trust. It is true that he had trouble expressing himself about anything personal, but I felt very sure that the caring was there. I just thought I would hear about it eventually.

David: I am certain that I had the caring feelings, but the only way I could express them was toward animals and children. I couldn't express them to adults, not for a long time. But as I learned to express my appreciation and caring to Vera, I grew better at it and came to see that by itself it created a very warm and loving environment for our relationship.

Vera: And I also saw that he was a very generous person, especially toward the "down and out" type person, generous with his time as well as his money. He was always supporting someone who had no way to succeed in society, even those on the very margin of society—perhaps even on their way to jail without his efforts to help them. And I saw this generosity as a way of expressing a very good quality and one that I admired. I still do. He is a true intellectual but also a man who believes in putting his ideas to work.

David: I am the kind of person that has to test out what I believe. My beliefs and my ideals have to work out in the crucible of life for me to trust their validity. That was true when I was growing up and it is still true today.

My philosophies toward the marriage experience have to be proved in people's lives in order for me to trust in their validity. When I see them working in the lives of couples, that is when I know they are true. And the quickest way to see couple growth is when they start expressing affirmation to each other.

Bobbye: So, after the contract is made—we will agree to a Mutual Commitment to Growth—couples can benefit from self-disclosure, shared meaning, and affirmation?

David: Yes. But it all begins with the *Mutual Commitment to Growth*. When that is in place, couples have the confidence to share, to disclose, to listen, to practice clear communication, to face clashes of wishes, and, yes, to affirm.

The Mutual Commitment to Growth was the "door" to the Maces' couple ideal about becoming each other's "close companion" throughout life. This ideal of "close companions" continues to be relevant. It was also the focus of a recent study by Dr. Robert Levenson of The University of California at Berkeley, published in the *AARP magazine* in an article about sex relations for seniors.

Dr. Levenson studied marriages of more than fifty years that had grown into "deep companionship, friendship, respect, and support." His conclusion at the end of his lengthy study was encouraging to couples willing to go through the "door" and work throughout their lives together for growth in their relationship: "Hang in there for the last chapters," he said. "They'll be good."

The Woods' Experience with Growth and Change

One clear advantage of agreeing to the Mutual Commitment to Growth is the freedom and confidence it gives couples to speak up about their opinions, feelings, and interpretations of spoken messages. Of course, there are going to be differences, but with the contract for growth in place, there is also the admission that even differences can lead to new understandings.

Several summers ago, Britton and Bobbye were at a camp in New Mexico, and their lodge's hostess had made an apricot cobbler for lunch. As the group went into the lounge to sit and enjoy the bowls of cobbler, Britton asked Bobbye, "Do you have a spoon?"

Bobbye interpreted the question to mean "Do you have a spoon for me to eat my cobbler with, like a good wife should provide?" She objected to the question and said so. Britton insisted that it was just a polite question about a utensil which he thought she would need. "I already had a spoon," he said.

Bobbye did not back down, however, from her interpretation. It led to a long conversation about how words could be heard differently than they might have been intended. But still the two points of view remained, as well as a definite emotional distance.

Because of the Mutual Commitment to Growth, the conversation continued throughout the afternoon. Finally, Bobbye asked in a teary voice, "Do you have a handkerchief?" Britton reached into his pocket and handed it to her. "Aha!" she said gleefully. "You thought that I was asking you to provide your handkerchief. That's what I thought earlier about the spoon."

The Woods were then able to discuss the issue (even with some laughter) and to admit that as with most things that happen in a couple relationship, there are really two points of view. Each person might like it if there were just one, but it simply isn't true. Finding out the partner's point of view can often be instructive and free us from assuming that everyone will agree with us if only we express our point of view in the clearest possible way.

Because of their Mutual Commitment to Growth, both Bobbye and Britton were able to say what they believed had happened. Both were able to voice their opinions and eventually to deal with the issue without resentment or secret grudges. They were even able to discern that part of the problem was that Britton had been traveling, and they needed some time together. That such honest and analytical conversations can happen is one of the advantages of the commitment to growth and change.

Couple Exercise

In many ways, the marital life journey can be an exciting trip into the future. Considering your journey as an adventure, share the answers to the following questions.

1. What is one memorable thing you have already shared? (e.g., a great vacation, a special celebration, etc.)
2. Describe a "souvenir" of your journey together (e.g., a ticket stub to a shared event, a special photograph, etc.).
3. In one sentence, describe your life partner, being sure to have at least one complimentary quality.
4. How would you define the term "close companion"?

David and Vera Mace Photo Album

1933

David and Vera Wedding, in London, July 26, 1933

1950s

Mace Family sitting down in front of their Madison, N.J. house in the early 1950s with, left to right, Vera, David, Fiona & Sheila.

1959

David and Vera on the Queen Elizabeth, on August 11, 1959 (probably coming or going from England to the US).

1960s

NCFR Pioneers: David and Vera Mace, Marion Hill, Ruth Hathaway Jewson, Evelyn M. Duvall.

1970s

David and Sarah Catron with David Mace, NY Eve party

1970s

David and Vera with Sarah Catron, the ACME Executive Director at that time.

1980s

David and Vera standing in front of their Black Mountain home where Bobbye and Britton Wood held their interviews.

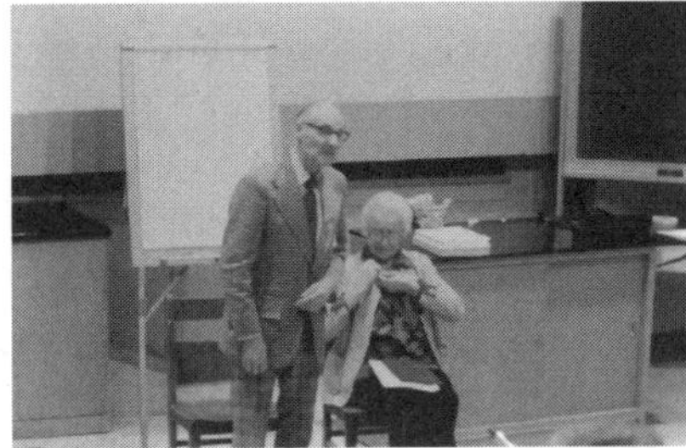

1980s

David/Vera leading Wake Forest Retreat

1988

Leon & Antoinette Smith, Father Calvo and David & Vera Mace at Atlanta International Conference, April 1988.

1994

Vera speaking on August 9th, 1994, in Black Mountain, North Carolina. She, on behalf of David and Vera's work; was receiving an award from a conference in Europe from the United Nations during the International Year of the Family, which she had not be able to attend.

Strength 2

A Communication Style that Works

Two cups with the silhouettes of David and Vera were gifts during the Mace Phonathon to encourage Daily Couple Talk.

Chapter 5

The Philosophy of a Communication Style that Works

Communication was the first "tool" that the Maces developed as a part of their Primary Coping System. This was a "tool," they believed, that would help a couple reach the goals they set in the flexible contract called the Growth Plan. Communication is valuable, much like a diamond.

Consider four "c's" as properties of the diamond.

The First "C" Is for "Cut."

The cut of a diamond is distinctive and represents all the various points of view in the diamond itself, sometimes referred to by jewelers as a prism. The prism, the cut, is what lets in light, rather like communication itself. Also, like the diamond, communication "shapes" and cuts must depend on the backstories of both the person and the stone.

Some people are raised in families where they are expected to converse as a duty, or at least as a form of etiquette. Meals, for example, are used at times for family communication, for processing the day and sharing one's experiences during it. Everyone around the dining table is supposed to talk AND listen. Some parents even forbid any electronics during the meal, so highly do they regard the art of conversation.

A few persons come from households where the conversation is unnecessary because all social interactions are done to the accompaniment of TV. Often there is no dining table to sit around. Everyone eats on the run while consulting an electronic source of some kind. Some people come from backgrounds where conversation at dinnertime is largely guided by a dominating or controlling figure with whom everyone else is expected to agree. Arguments can happen easily, so the people with these backstories learn that it's safer overall to tune out when others talk.

In other words, the "cut" and shape of our abilities to express ourselves in conversation largely depends on personality and backstory. These "cuts" often accompany us into marriage, where we can be surprised to learn that we now live with someone who has entirely different experiences. Sometimes there are even the difficulties of other relationships with their own sets of communication interaction that have created a special prism of interpretation and assumptions.

It is at this point over time where for growth and happiness to happen for a couple, conversational adjustments will have to be made. Communication is the primary way we get to know others and let them know us, so the "cut" or shape of our preferences and habits is extremely important.

The Second "C" Stands for "Clarity"

A diamond may be mined or made in a laboratory; it may be rare or suited only for chips in inexpensive jewelry. The greater the clarity, however, the more valuable the diamond.

Communication between partners is similar. To be valuable and to move the couple toward mutual understanding, clarity, when we talk, is important. Communication is one of the ways we let people know what is important to us. This is especially true of the marriage relationship, where a good communication system often becomes the measurement of how well a couple is doing.

Those who have never experienced the kind of couple education that Marriage Enrichment provides concerning communication skills are often skeptical of the value of this "tool." The Woods had this idea confirmed when they were in Perth, Australia, on a speaking tour. They had told the host of the planned event that in addition to their conversations with each other, they would be asking couples in the audience to share with their partner in a guided dialogue that evening. The alarmed host explained that the Asian couples in the audience would find the dialogue experience outside their cultural comfort zone and would not do it.

Yet, on that evening, when the Woods introduced the communication exercise, the Asian couples participated along with everyone else. Just before the Woods left Perth, an older Asian couple, who had been present that evening, gave them a thank-you card expressing appreciation for the new "tool" of couple dialogue and said they would be practicing it every day over tea. In the thank-you card was $100 in American currency. It is never too late for the kind of clarity that a good talk can bring.

The Third "C" Stands for "Color"

There are many choices in diamonds available to suit different tastes: yellow diamonds, traditional diamonds, chocolate diamonds, to name only a few. Colors fit the wide market of shoppers, as well as the prices those shoppers wish to pay, and advertisers spend lavishly to interest shoppers in the color choices.

Marriage is where an individual taste or "color" matters greatly, where recognizing our individual styles of talking and listening can be a life-long rewarding accomplishment. It is where the "color" of those styles of talking and listening can be amended or altered as we learn from each other what will work and what will not. In fact, in the marriage relationship, those couples who learn how to talk candidly, affirmingly, and intimately are those who experience the greatest feelings of closeness and support.

Like diamonds, words have color. Words can bless or defeat. They can encourage or create a prison that is so difficult to break free of that some people never do. Freedom can happen, but it takes time and practice. Words can inspire a nation at war; they can wound. Words can paint our everyday environments with the bright colors of joy or turn every personal landscape gray and dull. And in marriage, life's closest relationship of love, words can be a "tool" to build a wall or a bridge.

The Final "C" Is for "Carat"

The carat determines the value, the quality, and the weight of the diamond. The carat is what ultimately affects the cost of the stone and many times even the choice of a setting that will best showcase a particular diamond.

Like the diamond, communication often determines the value and quality of the relationship to the people in it. There may be little of value left in the relationship, even if there is a family at stake:

- if the couple has stopped having anything but superficial conversations,
- if the couple gives no time to share feelings and philosophies,
- if the couple no longer listens to each other's opinions or preferences.

The quality of the communication quite often becomes the decision-maker in whether to continue in the marriage for many couples. Like the diamond, communication is valuable in revealing what we want in life and what we are willing to do in order to get it.

According to Dr. David Olson, the designer of the famous inventory called Prepare and Enrich, "The communication item found to be most predictive of happily married couples was whether partners agree that they are satisfied with how they talk to each other."

One afternoon the Maces talked candidly with each other about their views on love. Here is what they said about the importance of communication in partners' life-events, dreams, desires, and efforts:

Britton: Let's talk about the subject of love.

David: Well, that may be hard to do. Love is a vast subject—sweet and sticky, hard to encompass. The story is told about an elderly man in the lowlands of Scotland, who went to church one morning alone. His wife Jenny was not with him, and when he went home for lunch after church, she asked him what the service was like. He gave a very noncommittal reply, and she asked, "What was the preacher's subject?" "He preached about love," the man said. "Oh," his wife said, "What was it like?" "Well, the best I could tell, it was like a flea struggling in a barrel of molasses."

What this old story is telling us is that there are many kinds of love and many different stages. The media might want us to dwell on only the sweet parts, but there are developmental processes of love, which we all have to go through from infancy, through puberty, through sexual attraction, through caring and concern.

This is the kind of unfolding growth and development that humans experience as they move to self-acceptance and eventually to be able to affirm and accept others. It is when this last stage develops, that we are best able to enter into marriage, for we have ourselves settled on what we want in life and on how to communicate that want to others.

Britton: I like that idea—that only when we are able to affirm and accept others and their ideas are we are able to be a couple, that we are able to love. I think one characteristic of a healthy love is that it does not tend to isolate you from other persons.

David: It can be most unhealthy when one person wants to spend every waking moment with the other. In fact, that is not love; that is insecurity. The partners that snoop on each other are not the partners that know each other well and have confidence in each other.

It's the ones that DON'T know each other that want to spy and insist on knowing every detail about something. They are watching and snooping on each other because the inner relationship has never developed. They never talk to each other about their ideas and feelings, so they know very little about the person they are married to. They barely know important things about themselves, so they stay away from conversations about values and dreams.

When a relationship is really close in the best sense of the word, that is, the relationship that gives each other total freedom to develop. Only when you truly love someone, you can send him or her in the direction of the development the other wants, even if it is not what you want. But those ideas of development are revealed to us through many conversations. Couples cannot help each other if they don't discuss their goals and ideas.

Vera: But aren't you really talking about sacrificial love? Isn't the act of helping your partner accomplish something that he or she really wants (but you may not) an example of sacrificial love?

David: I don't think there is such a thing as sacrificial love. I think it is the mature love that is capable of making a sacrifice. Mature love is the ability to free the other person to become whatever they feel is important for them to be. Then making sacrifices for that person is not a burden but a joy. Just like scraping up the money to put your kids through college is gladly done if you are proud of their development.

Vera: I think this is just a matter of semantics. Love is making sacrifices. Couples make sacrifices for each other every day, and the motivation for doing so is love.

David: I guess it comes back to the old issue of altruism. I don't think there is really such a thing. The people who act altruistically do so because it is satisfying to them. They are measuring up to an ideal that they have for themselves. They are demonstrating their own principles, watching themselves do it, and perhaps even applauding themselves.

I mean even in the final page of Dickens' *Tale of Two Cities,* Sidney Carlton is telling himself that he is doing something noble, something he may be remembered for, even after the mess he has made of his life.

Bobbye: "It's a far, far better thing that I do"? "It's a far, far better place that I go to?"

David: Yes. He is finally able to get outside himself, and with one supreme experience to reach his goal for himself. He died gladly. With one great, final leap, he is arriving at his ideal.

Vera: But wasn't that sacrificial?

David: I would say that it was self-fulfillment for Carlson. He told himself that it was a "better thing," but he was also meeting some need in his own nature. It could be for both reasons, you know.

Vera: I think he was subscribing to the ideal "to give and not to count the cost." Isn't that what love does?

David: I would say yes, but you are talking about the outward cost. I think there is a compensating factor inside that makes his sacrifice worthwhile. A sacrifice can be a joy if it is willingly offered for something you strongly believe in. And his was.

Love is complicated, and love for one's ideals and principles is one facet of it, just like love for another person. And both are examples of mature love, love that is able to take one outside oneself. But you can at the same time demonstrate your own principles and your love for them, while you are making a sacrifice for someone whom you love. The two are not mutually exclusive.

Vera: What about Jean Valjean in *Les Misérables*? He was so changed by the selflessness of the Bishop who saved him from prison that he spent the rest of his life giving to others what they most needed. Wouldn't that be an example of sacrificial love? Valjean was someone who even risked himself at the barricades to rescue the young revolutionary whom his daughter had fallen in love with. Isn't that sacrificial?

David: Yes, we could get example after example from the literature of sacrificial love. I'm just saying that there can be more than one motivation for it. And there can be more than one reward for what you are doing. *Love is a complex relationship, and we should expect life's most important quality to be complex.*

I think what both of us are saying here is that in literature and in marriage, there has to be a return of some kind for your love. In marriage, there should be a responsive return. In the ordinary, everyday marriage, you cannot expect a sacrifice every day for you. There must be a balance.

There may be periods or crises in a marriage where you must hold on without return, but in the everyday life of the marriage there must be the response for your love, a kind of give and take. And it is through communication that we make clear what the terms of that give and take should be. That's the key to growth, right there. You talk about it. You talk about it often.

The Woods' Experience with a Communication Style that Works

Sweet words have the power to restore sagging spirits and tired bodies and to reveal the exact emotion that can change moods.

After an unusually stressful day, the Bobbye and Britton gratefully went to bed, exhausted from dealing with misbehaving appliances, a leak in their roof, and discouraging news about a serious family illness. For a while, they just lay side by side, digesting the day and its somewhat overwhelming complications. But just before turning out the light, Britton looked at Bobbye and quietly said, "You are my girl." She turned to look at him. "And I am your guy," he said.

These were exactly the right words to begin a brief conversation about the day and its difficult events. They changed the feelings of discouragement and fatigue, lightening the mood that a minute before had dominated the whole bedroom. They reminded both that no matter what else was happening, the relationship was secure and ways to manage circumstances would be found. They restored perspective and steadied both partners.

Couple communication is imperative to a growing and loving relationship. And when the words are right, they have the power to remind a couple of the profound importance of that fact.

Couple Exercise
(Designed by the Maces)

Score the following typical couple categories from one to ten, with ten being high. Score the relationship, not yourself and not your partner. Score where you think the relationship is now, not where you wish it would be. When you have scored all ten categories, add the totals. This represents the potential you have already achieved. Discuss any differences that might need clarification.

COMMON GOALS AND VALUES ____________

COMMITMENT TO GROWTH ____________

COMMUNICATION SKILLS ____________

CREATIVE USE OF CONFLICT ____________

APPRECIATION AND AFFECTION ____________

AGREEMENT ON GENDER ROLES ____________

COOPERATION AND TEAMWORK ____________

SEXUAL FULFILLMENT ____________

MONEY MANAGEMENT ____________

DECISION MAKING ____________

TOTALS ____________

Chapter 6

Affirmation, Hope, and the Silver Thread of Romance

Several years ago, Bobbye and Britton heard marriage counselors Harville Hendrix and Helen Hunt speak candidly at a conference about the power of affirmation in a close relationship such as marriage. The speakers were relating what had happened to them at an earlier stage of their relationship, when they were unable to deal with their mutual unhappiness together and were at the point of divorce.

Worried about the impact on the many couples whom they had already befriended and helped, they shared their distress with a trusted friend. The friend listened carefully and then asked them to spend a weekend at his mountain retreat before they made any final plans. The retreat would be for just the two of them and it would be free. They accepted.

The friend said that there was only one rule for the weekend: there was to be NO criticism of any kind, not even criticism disguised as an "observation," a "suggestion," or a witty "comment." They were to talk to each other about subjects that interested them, and they were to give compliments and affirmations freely for the whole weekend. They kept the rules.

At the end of the weekend, they were astonished to find that they felt much friendlier toward each other and much more hopeful about their relationship. They decided to postpone the divorce proceedings for a while and to explore the possibility of taking a vacation together with the same rules that they had abided by at the mountain retreat.

They also began a systematic analysis of what had driven them apart over time and what had happened that weekend that now made them feel hopeful. Too much criticism over too long a time, they learned, had been destructive to the relationship. Two professional people, two academic-minded people, two well-intentioned people had nevertheless fallen into the habit of criticizing each other and telling themselves the criticism was merely instructive and for the best.

Their experience is common to many couples, at least the criticism and its effect on the relationship. Too many couples never get to the healing of affirmation. Locked in conversations reporting the other's faults and flaws, pointing out all failures and mistakes, lecturing, demeaning, and sometimes mocking, the result to no one's surprise becomes distance, hostility, and resentment.

Dr. Charles and Dr. Elizabeth Schmitz, speakers at a Better Marriage conference, once reported the results of a similar discovery as they researched the habits of couples married for at least fifty years and who considered their marriage as successful. The Schmitzes have traveled to five continents, forty-nine countries, every state in the US, and seven provinces of Canada, asking couples with a long-term relationship about their opinions on what makes a successful marriage.

The top answer they received was the overwhelming importance of speaking kindly and courteously to each other, no matter what the subject under consideration. The Schmitzes thought couples should talk often about everything with each other—about health, about money, about sex, about family, about food, about fears and concerns. Staying connected verbally was critical to couple happiness, the Schmitzes found, and this was true around the world.

But the happiest couples were those who not only felt the freedom to discuss every subject but who also had learned to sprinkle all conversations with "we" and "our" and "us" and to act as each other's "cheerleader." That encouragement and affirmation resulted in each partner feeling strong as an individual, warm in support of the partner's goals and plans, and certain that each had a "voice" in all couple decisions and conflicts, a "voice" that would be heard, a "voice" that mattered.

Not only did the Schmitzes find that the affirming couples could navigate through all issues, including the difficult ones, but they also found that the top advice the fifty-year couples wanted to give to newlyweds was to be aware of how the newly married couples talked to each other. To keep self-identity and relationship strong, the Schmitzes advised couples embarking on the great adventure of marriage to stay affirming and encouraging. Do no harm with words, they said, and never discount the partner, never.

Marriage has many moving parts, and each unique couple must coordinate those parts, but *regular affirmation is one fundamental asset to a happy and long-term relationship.* With practice it becomes easier, even if it has not been a conversational habit in the past, and it pays rich dividends.

Like many marriage counselors, educators, and coaches since the 1970s, David and Vera found the power of affirmation to be liberating and productive in creating couple growth. Frequently, they even practiced an affirmation time in their speeches, to the delight of audiences. Affirmation became an integral part of Marriage Enrichment, and couples all over the world have been richer for it.

Here is what they said when Britton asked how they came to the whole approach of affirmation and structured couple encouragement:

> **David:** I gradually became aware that the language and literature of counseling were not affirmative and not positive. The emphasis in counseling had become diagnosis: find out what is wrong. I realized that this was not productive

of motivation for couples. In fact, it often produced discouragement verging on despair, a sudden feeling of having many problems and no clue about how to solve them.

Then I asked myself, what is it that gives couples the motivation to address their issues? What makes them ready to work their way out of a messy situation? In our Marriage Enrichment Groups (MEGs), I became aware of the tremendous power of modeling, enabling couples to see in another couple how a marriage can work.

Often distressed couples in our groups when seeing and hearing another couple discussing an important but divisive issue say to themselves, "Well, if they can do it, we can do it." And then comes motivation, and this motivation has its roots in a convinced state of mind that the couple themselves could address their issues. And this recognition produced hope. Then I saw that hope itself could produce the motivation. As long as people have hope, they struggle on, but when hope is gone, they give up.

When couples lose hope, they turn outward and begin to look for compensations in other places for what they failed to get in their marriage. That's one reason affairs come in, you see, or that's when the couple turns to their friends instead of to each other. When a couple no longer tries to address their marital issues with each other, this is a sign that hope has gone, and when hope has gone, motivation has gone.

So, through our group work, we began to have couples model ways they handled difficulties. They did not talk about their opinions or ideas; they talked about their experiences and feelings. In addition to the private dialogues that all couples had, we encouraged those who felt comfortable doing so to share with each other the practical ways they dealt with difficult issues, and to do so in the group. What we also began to notice was that many of these couples also said nice things to and about each other.

As we watched the new couples begin to be aware of what other couples were showing them, we also began to see hope in the other couples in the group. Then we saw the importance of the dream, the dream of a beautiful relationship, which like a silver thread has gone through the whole of recorded history. You will find that dream expressed in love stories, in folk tales, in legends, in songs, in poetry. But the most exciting thing about it is that the dream that has died in people can also be revived. We have watched it many times.

What Marriage Enrichment is doing for many couples is reviving their lost dreams, the dreams with which they went into marriage. And all these important things happen without couples saying anything to other couples about what is happening.

Some couples have given up because the marriage did not turn out to be the way they expected. They got stuck on some plateau of difficulty. They got stuck in criticism or in the kind of indifferent behavior that can mask a good bit of anxiety.

But what happens in Marriage Enrichment—and happens often enough that we are quite sure about this—is to revive the dream. It is the dream of beauty, of romance, of mutual affection, affirmation, and tenderness. It is the dream they thought that they had lost. It can be found again with affirming couples who offer a model of how to keep the relationship on a steady course of growth. It is an encouragement lacking in everyday society.

Vera: I came to this point in our philosophy from a different perspective. David came to this perspective from the field of counseling. I came to it from dealing with children. As a teacher, I was impressed over and over again with a child's responses to encouragement. Unless you can give a child encouragement and affirmation, you are just popping in information—even useful information—but you are not really educating.

Affirmation gives the child the awareness that he is whole, that he is appreciated for his good qualities, that it is OK to try new things—even OK to try them and fail. It is an awareness greatly needed in the whole of education.

And then from education, I applied this to marriage. Just as a good teacher tries to help a child believe in himself, and just as a good teacher encourages a sense of hope and expectation, Marriage Enrichment seeks to instill both confidence and expectation in a couple, bringing them to look into themselves for the solutions that could make them both happier.

It helps them to find those inner resources, to share them with each other, and move toward the recovery of hope for a better and more satisfactory relationship. *When there is hope, there is room for affirmation. When there is an affirmation, there is a climate that produces growth.*

Britton: I can remember one of our daughters standing on a chair and measuring herself to me and saying, "Look how big I am." All my daughters were looking forward to growth. And the only time they would either suck their thumb or get into some baby-like tone would be the time that they were not feeling affirmed. They felt put down, they felt a sense of low self-esteem, and they were not anticipating growth.

And this was contrary to their nature, as it is for all healthy young children. Unless something really serious has happened to them, their nature is to want to grow and to look forward to growing up and being independent. Many times, when asked their age a six-year-old child will say six and one/half. That extra half is important because it lets you know in their minds, they are almost seven. They are growing.

David: Yes, there are books that maintain that the main job of parenting is maintaining and increasing the child's self-esteem. And there are also studies—and there really have been very few, maybe four all totaled—about "well" families, healthy families, which define *the main ingredient of that family health is the fact that the families are continually affirming each other.*

Vera: Yes, they like each other, and they tell each other. And they keep on telling each other.

David: And therefore, they like being together. There's nothing better than constantly being affirmed by those you love.

Bobbye: When we attended one of your Marriage Enrichment seminars, we were much interested in a conversation that the two of you had on the stage. In the conversation, you exchanged statements showing what you especially appreciated about each other.

I had never seen anyone do that, and I enjoyed it very much. Then you had all the couples in the audience make the same kind of positive exchange, and it produced very good feelings and very hopeful feelings about our relationship.

We discovered that we could do the same conversation together at other times and produce the same good feelings that we had at the seminar. It has become a conversation that we try to have often, and it never fails to make both of us feel better about ourselves and about each other.

Britton: Where did you get the idea for this kind of conversation, this structure of affirmation and appreciation?

David: Hmm. We've been doing it for a very long time. But I think I got the idea about fifteen years ago in Tallahassee, Florida, when I attended a professional conference about parents and teenagers.

The speaker had the parents sitting in a circle with the teenagers. Each parent was to affirm their teenager, and the teenager was to affirm the parent also. At the end of the time, there were many tears as family members connected in sweet ways.

But as I was sitting in the audience, I thought that this might be a good thing to include in Marriage Enrichment. And from that time on, we have always included a time of affirmation in our programs. It was one of our early really important discoveries about the power of affirmation.

We started initially with just Vera and I affirming each other. Then we asked for volunteers who wanted to affirm each other in front of the group. Some couples liked that; some felt it was confrontational. So, then we had all couples do it privately at the same time. That worked best because there was no confrontation there; in fact, it became a very rewarding experience for everyone.

Affirmation costs nothing but it creates feelings of warmth and tenderness for the couple. And for couples who have been locked into a conversational style of criticism and distance, it especially feels good. In fact, it can lead to healing and hope.

Vera: I think society as a whole has not recognized the very great importance of kindness and tenderness. So many people are just starved for kindness and affirmation and suffer greatly for its lack. Kindness and affirmation say "Somebody cares about me. I count."

Britton: That is true. But some people have trouble with accepting affirmation. I personally have a hard time with it when nice words are said to me and often look for the motivation that would cause another person to say them. I can't seem to accept them at face value. I think that may be true for many others.

Bobbye: There is even a style of management where the employer always starts a meeting with an employee by giving a compliment before he or she ever gets around to the criticism or reprimand. Many employees just wait for the "but" following the compliment. No wonder many people feel uncomfortable or suspicious of affirmation.

David: Yes, and it's particularly true of the British. Compliments make them uncomfortable; it is just "not done." So, you have to be very careful when you are getting some honor in England. You can very easily leave the impression that you are vain and arrogant if you simply accept compliments and praise.

Vera: They call it "tooting your own trumpet."

David: Yes, the standard response is supposed to be "Don't mention it."

Bobbye: And in Mexico the proper response is "De nada," which means "It is nothing."

David: I have had problems myself with affirmation, following the British model. I wanted to shoo it away and turn the attention and the compliments back on the giver, not the gift. I have tried to change the model I grew up with in Scotland and to simply say "Thank you. That makes me feel good."

And it's the truth; it really does make me feel good. "Don't mention it" *is a fake!* All people need affirmation, and to get it regularly from someone you love and respect is merely good relational health.

Britton: Recount, if you will, some great affirmation that you have received.

David: Actually, it was the year when Brigham-Young University gave us both many accolades and honors for our contributions to families due to our work in Marriage Enrichment. At the ceremony, Vera was given an honorary doctorate. This was highly symbolic to me because she so richly deserved it. In 1943, when WWII was winding down and Vera came back to England from the US, I began to work again at the Marriage Guidance Council.

Vera went to work on her PhD while I did the counseling services. When she was about half through with her academic work, I became swamped with counseling needs and responsibilities. One legacy of the war was the extraordinary number of couples in serious trouble. So, Vera left the university and came to help me out. But she never got back to finish the PhD.

Getting the honorary doctor's degree after we had moved our family to the US was a great gift and symbolic of her unselfish help with my work at the Guidance Council.

That honorary degree made me feel that justice had been done. She deserved this and had for some time. She had made a very affirming gift to my work, and at last, she was being rewarded for her choices. Neither of us would have wanted to say, "Don't mention it."

Vera: Yes, I was very much rewarded and that's exactly how I saw it.

David: The whole awards ceremony was for our work in the field of marriage and family, and I knew that Vera deserved it as much as me. I loved watching her get hooded for the honorary doctorate. It was a joint affirmation.

Vera: The thing is that when we were first married, David could not look me in the eyes and tell me that he loved me. He was not comfortable sharing his feelings at all, but certainly not when others were present. But here in front of all these thousands of cheering people, he leaned down, congratulated me, complimented me, and kissed me. I still remember how happy and surprised I felt.

Britton: That was a great affirmation, all the more important because it was done in public.

David: Yes, what I say is that if I can learn to do it, anyone can.

Another famous marriage counselor and teacher, Dr. John Gottman, tells of his observations of couples who come to him for counseling. Dr. Gottman can sit in his office and listen to them for as little as fifteen minutes, he says, and accurately predict which couples will divorce, which will stay together but not be happy, and which will find ways to increase their love and support of each other throughout their years together.

The criteria for his prediction are simple: those couples who say something positive or affirming about or to each other while getting acquainted in the fifteen-minute session, those couples who use positive gestures (touches, pats, smiles), and those are the couples who have a better chance for success and satisfaction.

Those who use criticisms, complaints, lectures, sarcasm, manipulations, and gestures of contempt, distance, and disrespect (even during the fifteen minutes of conversation) are the couples who either will not stay in the marriage for long or who will not be able to be happy with each other if they do stay married.

Affirmation is more than a mere pleasant experience. It is life-affirming and makes a difference in the quotient of happiness a couple will experience. Just as true courtesy is deeper than mere etiquette and can set the tone for a caring and giving relationship, so regular affirmation enriches the daily climate of living.

Affirmation can have surprising results, as a local newspaper article revealed. It told of an old school bus which pulled up to a football stadium one September evening, full of boys from a nearby state reform school ready to play a game. To the astonishment of the boys inside, they saw a line of adults cheering for them as they exited the old bus. They knew nobody in the rival high school and did not know that some of the parents there had learned that these boys played in their jeans and worn-out jerseys and shoes, with not even enough equipment for both offense and defense. The team had no cheerleaders and few fans.

The rival high school parents had decided to correct that issue, even if for only one evening. They sat behind the state school bench, cheered by name when a player did well, and congratulated on good passes and touchdowns. When the game was over, they even stood outside the bus and wished the boys well for their next game.

The surprise was what happened afterward. As the parents followed up with some new equipment and new uniforms for the state school football team, they also learned that most of the boys had never heard their name called out with praise attached to it. Many of them had never received either a compliment or a gift. They certainly had never been cheered for.

The parents' actions became a catalyst for improved behavior among the boys on the football team and for some of them reduced sentences for better behavior. Affirmation thus led to general life improvement.

The Woods' Experience with Affirmation

Bobbye: We took a trip several years ago from Dallas to California with our three teenaged daughters and my mother. And on that trip, I tried an exercise in group dynamics that turned out to be very revealing.

We were on our first day out when the air conditioner quit working in our new car. In July, in West Texas, we stopped at several garages to get the car fixed, but it was too new to be repaired by the mechanics where we stopped. No one could do it. Each mechanic assured us that if we just went on to the next big town, someone there could help us.

One dealer finally was able to find the right part, and at last, we made it to our first night's accommodations in El Paso. But by the next morning, everyone was already tired and cross. Hardly we were back in the car when the criticisms began. "She's hogging all the air conditioning, as usual."

"She's got her feet on my pillow." "This car is too cold, and I don't have a sweater." "Are we almost there?" "This trip is too long."

So, I suggested that we play a game. Each person in the car was to think of one good thing about every other person in the car and tell that person. "Would you like to play that game?" I asked. The idea was not received very well, in fact, with a resounding "NO," but as the mother, I prevailed, and we made a tentative beginning.

Britton: But an interesting thing was the emotional insecurity at that point. Each of the children was doubtful that anyone would think of something good to say about them. They each knew how they had been behaving. They each knew that the climate in the car had not lent itself to affirmation or compliments of any kind.

Bobbye: We started with Britton, and not only did everyone think of something good to say about him, but as we went in order of the seating arrangement around the car, the things we said about each person got longer and longer. We all found more positive things to say about each other, things that probably had needed to be said for a long time.

There were tears and statements like, "I didn't know you thought THAT," and then there were hugs. And then everyone wanted to do it one more time. We played the "game" for about forty-five minutes, and a family that thought it was loving and affirming learned that it had been a long time since they had actually said loving and affirming things to each other.

The verbal exchanges and responses turned out to be very positive, and when they had finished, it had produced such warm feelings that it made traveling much more enjoyable for everyone. It changed the mood in the car. It set a new tone for the whole family trip.

Britton: And another wonderful side effect was that everyone became agreeable to carry their own luggage. As the only male in the car, I especially appreciated that.

Bobbye: So, one thing we learned from this experience was that both of us needed to be much more verbal with each other about the things we like and appreciate. Hearing good feelings about ourselves and expressing good feelings about each other are important. So are good feelings expressed often to family members?

Couple Exercise

Each person should think of three things he or she likes and appreciates about the partner. Often, we say thank you or some word of appreciation about what someone DOES rather than IS. In this exercise, think of the quality or characteristic that you especially are grateful for, and say so. Three qualities; three expressions of gratitude and affirmation. Take turns sharing with each other.

Chapter 7

The Value of Daily Couple Talk

Couples who devise a way to talk to each other that leads to understanding are couples who watch their relationship prosper over time. Couples who regularly carve out of their busy schedules a time every day to talk to each other—talk specifically about their relationship, how it is faring, and how they feel about it—these are the very couples who make giant strides in growth and more intimate connections.

All the experts in the field of marriage agree on the importance of daily couple talk time, although they call it by different names. One of the earliest organizations to give couple talk time a name was Marriage Encounter, who called it a "10 and 10." This meant that there would be ten minutes of writing about one's thoughts and feelings and ten minutes of a quiet reading of what each partner had written. After each partner has had time to reflect on the other's feelings and ideas, the couple then would discuss the list, if they desired. Most couples today prefer a verbal exchange, as well as a written, but the "10 and 10" has long been a staple for couples.

The Association for Couples in Marriage Enrichment (ACME), founded by David and Vera in 1973 and now called Better Marriages, refers to this talking process as the *Daily Sharing Time,* a time for partners to discuss feelings and ideas, worries and aspirations, philosophies and special memories. Its goal is to keep each other current, as well as strengthening the couple relationship.

Dr. John Gottman calls it the fifteen-Minute Talk Time, and from the vantage point of his long career in counseling, teaching, and research, he assures couples that it will make immediate differences in the quality of their relationship and even improve their sex life.

Dr. John Van Epp calls it a couple "huddle" and recommends its use in the same way that sports teams gather for planning, assignments, and encouragement. Very few relationships stay balanced on their own, according to Dr. Van Epp and his daughter Dr. Morgan Cutlip, and the "huddle" is a simple way to deal regularly with everyday issues. Like the Daily Sharing Time, the goal of the "huddle" is strengthening the couple relationship.

Dr. Scott Stanley, one of the founders of the organization called Prevention and Relationship Enhancement Program (PREP), has designed a very effective couple Speaker/Listener Technique for times of important discussion in a couple's relationship. Whoever is the designated speaker has the "floor" (sometimes even holding in one hand a visual symbol of a "floor"). The speaker gets to briefly state his or her position on whatever topic the couple needs to pursue. Then he or she pauses.

The listener's job is to paraphrase the speaker's words he or she heard without challenging or editing. This procedure continues until the speaker has fully disclosed his or her position. Then the "floor" is exchanged, and it becomes the turn of the listener to be the speaker. As a couple takes turns covering a subject by speaking AND listening, new insights on the issue emerge and new understandings are often created. Once both have fully shared, each partner knows the other's perspective and also feels their perspective has been heard.

A shared responsibility gives both partners a turn at being both speaker and listener, thus building communication skills. If the technique is used regularly, it gives more practice of this useful skill for times when attitudes toward a subject are in conflict and both voices must be heard in order to make a good decision.

Many other organizations now use this communication technique, calling it active listening, reflective listening, or mirroring. One person even refers to it as the "Drive-Through Technique," suggesting Fast Food Drive-Through lanes where orders are given over an outside microphone and repeated by a staff member inside whose job is to clarify the order so that both persons are attuned to what food is expected.

Although the techniques for daily sharing or practicing communication skills are slightly different from each other, as are the names by which they are called, the organizations are all in agreement that *this form of communication can be central to the couple's growth in shared meaning and in developing understanding.*

After many years of participating in their own conversational ritual which they called the *Daily Sharing Time*, this is what the Maces said about daily couple-talk:

> ***Bobbye:*** Let's talk for just a minute about the subject of communication. Britton asked earlier why it was so difficult for some couples to talk to each other about their relationship; I think he used the word "barriers."
>
> What in your experience makes it difficult for couples to talk to each other in an intimate or personal way?
>
> ***David:*** Basically, to a greater or lesser degree, I think they are just not yet open to the importance of daily communication with each other. They have not yet seen its value, and sometimes find it awkward just to get started.
>
> And for other couples, I think that a block is almost always caused by the fact that one of them or perhaps both of them have

defenses up regarding something that has happened in the past. They are on guard against opening up their inner selves to each other. Perhaps they feel guilty about something; perhaps they are afraid of being hurt or taken advantage of in some way.

I think when two people can be open with themselves, they should not have difficulty in dialoguing with each other. It is the presence of defenses that keep them too cautious to even find the words to say. *They are trying to protect their inner selves from each other, and yet this is exactly the area that they need to explore and share.*

When we are working with couples in our groups, we always try to help by making them proceed with easy steps. We get them not to focus on the past—the way things WERE—and not in the future. We ask them to keep their attention on where they are at the moment, the thoughts and the feelings that they are experiencing just then. This technique works in the group process, and it could work with reluctant couples who want to talk about their relationship in the privacy of their own homes.

Vera: And in our groups, we emphasize the importance of listening. Dialogue is not just about speaking; it is also a matter of listening. All of us can pick up on the clues that someone doesn't want to talk. It's harder to tell when someone simply does not want to listen. For example, I can be here but not ready to hear.

Britton: That's very good, very insightful.

Bobbye: What about the two of you? Would you know, David, if she stopped listening to you?

David: I would know. I would sense it by the way she was looking at something else or turning in another direction. It would be shown in her demeanor and attitude. I would assume from that as she was preoccupied and not willing or ready to listen at that moment.

Bobbye: And what would you do?

David: I would ask, "Do you not want to talk now? Is there something on your mind?" This gives her a way to let me know that she is not ready to talk at that time. She would probably then tell me when would be a better time, and I would feel fine about it because then I would know that her mind is occupied with some other task. I would know that I will eventually learn about what is on her mind. I can wait without wondering what is really going on.

Britton: So, another of the barriers to a couple dialogue sometimes is timing, in addition to the barrier of fear about revealing something personal and thus making them feel vulnerable.

David: Yes, but there is also the matter of inclination. A person may tell themselves that they don't have the time for a couple sharing when they really mean they don't have the inclination. It's like the wife staying up late at night doing tasks because she doesn't want to have sex. She stays busy with some household task until she is sure the husband has gone to sleep.

Making excuses to avoid having a couple sharing time is a form of evasion, but one can assuage guilt by saying to himself or herself that there are things to do right now. Couple sharing time is a matter of priority and both need to recognize it. Getting in the habit of the Daily Sharing Time is a discipline both partners must honor in order to get anything out of it.

The Daily Sharing Time is where you share your thoughts, wishes, intentions, and feelings. It is not really a dialogue—a back-and-forth kind of conversation. Each person at a time does the sharing; then it is the other person's turn. It should not be extended past a twenty-minute time, and both should stick with that time limit and not abuse it. *The Daily Sharing Time* is simply a time for getting in tune with each other.

Vera: And it is helpful to have it at the same time every day. *Each situation is different as is each couple,* but a certain amount of discipline about sticking to a schedule is important.

David: Yes, we have found that early in the morning is the best time for us. I get up and make tea, which I bring to Vera in bed. Then as we drink our tea, we start the day by sharing our feelings and thoughts about where we are. It centers us for the day by drawing us closer to each other.

We started out with the Marriage Encounter process of writing down our feelings and ideas into some kind of list, but now we just talk. There is no order to who shares first and there is no ritual. It is a simple process. But the Daily Sharing Time is for keeping us close as a couple with knowledge about what is currently going on within each of us.

Here is what I have observed the importance of the Daily Sharing Time, which is one of the ways many couples participate in Marriage Enrichment. In fact, getting into Marriage Enrichment has at least four typical steps:

1. A couple attends some introductory session, a program or a retreat. They get some specific insights and some lessons about growth. They might even make out a growth plan since these are all individually done to suit the needs and the interests of each couple. They might choose to attend some other meeting because of their initial interest, but this is the starting place for many couples.
2. The second way that many couples maintain an interest in continuing involvement in Marriage Enrichment is by the use of the Daily Sharing Time, a plan for keeping continuously in touch with each other day by day. If a couple has attended a group meeting or two, but they don't do this simple couple interaction, it's easy to fall back into misunderstandings and hurt feelings. The Daily Sharing Time clears the air and puts both on the same page, and it happens with

such a regularity that both can feel its results immediately. This is very helpful for those couples who were reluctant at first to try it.

3. The third way that keeps couples involved is the real dialogue, where couples make an appointment with each other to use an anger technique in order to deal with the obstacles and difficulties that are a part of life. This will be the back-and-forth conversation, where negotiation happens after there is an understanding of where each person is on a particular issue and perhaps even a new understanding of why this is so. Expressing feelings that lie behind the issue is an important way to cast the obstacles and difficulties in a new light.
4. The fourth thing is to agree to be in a MEG for a year. Here couples make themselves accountable to share their own ongoing growth with the group and to listen to other couples explaining their own couple progress.

We say that these four items will get a couple into the Marriage Enrichment pattern. We believe that if a couple will stick with these items and practice them, they will be pleased with the noticeable progress they are experiencing.

But here is the really astonishing part. We have seen this often enough now that we know it to be true. The most common item for a couple to give up is the Daily Sharing Time. The very thing that they need the most is the thing they let go of.

Then when a couple begins to let that go, to stop staying current with each other about where each is in their thoughts and feelings, that is when they also begin to let misunderstandings pile up again and discouragement to set in.

They may even continue to attend a group, but if they are not doing the Daily Sharing Time, they lose sight of the couple growth gains they have made. And other couples will notice it too.

Britton: What is the prognosis for couples who do the four steps?

David: Oh, it's good. Very, very good. If there is something terribly wrong, it would have come out in the group, and they would have dealt with it there. If there were rifts in the relationship so deep as to cause divorce, those rifts would have become apparent as they practiced the four steps over time.

The couple would then have resolved the issues causing the rift and they would continue practicing the steps. In fact, we know very few couples in all the years that we have dealt with groups who have actually divorced. It happens, but it is far, far below the national average for divorce.

Bobbye: How did the two of you discover the value of the Daily Sharing Time? Did you start it because of your philosophy, or did your philosophy come from the activity of doing it?

Vera: We have been doing it for many, many years in a variety of forms. Once upon a time, we even called it the Quiet Time. It is practiced in a variety of forms by the Quakers.

David: But our present technique of the Daily Sharing Time really came from Marriage Encounter, as we said. We tried to meet their daily standards and found them to be very helpful for our own relationship. Actually, we had done sharing times together before that because we believed in them, but they had just been hit or miss.

It was when we developed a fixed time with rules about what we did and what we said that we immediately noticed a change. We no longer make lists of our feelings and mental moods, as I said, but the effect on us is dramatic. The Daily Sharing Time only takes twenty minutes, and we do stick to that time frame, but we simply couldn't get along without it.

We share our general emotional states and feelings. If there are any negative feelings we have about yesterday, or any apprehensions we have about today, we share those. *It is a checking-in process, both with ourselves and with each other,* but it helps us know where each other is for that day, and that information alone is invaluable.

The Woods' Experience with the Daily Sharing Time

Bobbye came to marriage from a family that did not share feelings with each other. Furthermore, as a girl, she caught the idea that only good moods and good feelings were appropriate for her to share. If something went well at school on a particular day, for example, that could be shared at the dinner table.

If it did not go well, that information was to be kept private, because it was no one else's concern and certainly not of interest to the family in general. It might have been a typical family background, but it was not particularly helpful for finding personal feelings and participating in a Daily Sharing Time, a time that both Bobbye and Britton deemed to be important in their couple growth.

In Britton's family, as the third child and the first son, there was also talk around the dinner table, but no one asked Britton how he felt about any subject. As a result, Britton had no experience in sharing feelings. With his friends in the growing up years, he was the one who listened and learned what they felt. He was not in the habit of sharing personal information with others.

So, when he was dating Bobbye and they were talking about the possibility of marriage, Bobbye said, "You have not even told me that you love me." Both saw that personal communication would be needed, but neither had had the background that made it easy to share.

After they got married, they worked on having a good relationship, although they still lacked the communication skills they later learned in Marriage Enrichment. When the Woods learned from the Maces about the value of the Daily Sharing Time, they were intrigued but perplexed about how to actually do it.

They began by just asking each other, "Do you have time for a sharing time this morning?" If the answer was yes, then Britton would get some half sheets of paper and both would write "I Feel" at the top of the page. Then each would write three feelings they had at that moment and share the paper with each other. Some days they talked together about the feelings; some days they didn't. Some days they did no sharing at all and felt its lack all through the day.

The Woods did this method of sharing feelings for several months. Gradually they became more adept at discovering what each person felt, and finally, they could share their feelings with each other without the need for writing. They trained themselves to become more self-aware and to share that awareness. It was a new discovery and one that led to a close connection as a couple. Now no day goes by without this one way of staying current and close.

Couple Exercise

Here are some questions for couple talk regarding communication. Each partner should answer the questions, and then check with the other person to see whether you got the answer correct. The point is not the accuracy of the answer; the point is information for discussion.

Questions About My Partner:

1. Who is someone my partner admires?
2. What is my partner's favorite food?
3. Where did my partner go to First Grade?
4. What would my partner like to do if he/she had a totally free day?
5. How does my partner express love and affection for me?

Questions About My Partner's Family:

1. Who is my partner's favorite relative?
2. How does my partner's family celebrate birthdays or other important occasions?
3. How does my partner's family show love and affection?
4. What are the names of my partner's grandparents, and what does he or she call them?
5. How does my partner's family deal with conflict?

Questions About Our Relationship:

1. Who is the better listener, me or my partner? Why?
2. How well do we communicate feelings to each other?
3. Do we generally agree on how to spend our money?
4. What is my partner likely to do when we disagree?
5. How can we spend more time talking together?

Chapter 8
Processing Feelings

At a recent MEG meeting, every table of couples identified "better speaking and listening skills" as the single most important thing couples need for a better relationship. They picked "better speaking and listening skills" from a list of items couples would profit from using, for example:

- sharing power;
- demonstrating goals and values;
- using good problem-solving techniques;
- showing appreciation;
- managing money well; and
- expressing feelings.

Their choice of speaking and listening skills was not surprising, given the results of many national surveys and research grants studying the quality of couple life. Most of those studies in fact find communication as the number one issue that determines whether a couple is happy or not, so it was not particularly surprising that every table of couples picked "speaking and listening." What is surprising about the couples' decision is that their second choice for improving daily couple life was "expressing feelings."

Expressing the feelings attached to an issue under dispute is an essential part of the Anger Contract, a contract examined and recommended in the third part of the Primary Coping System, which is called a Creative Use of Conflict. Expressing feelings regarding a subject of disagreement may be a difficult step, but it is important. Often, the feelings about the issue are a part of the issue itself. To pretend that a discussion of feelings is not needed is to miss relevant information. Reaching a sensible resolution to a hot topic without exploring the feelings involved may be like trying to measure temperature with a ruler. It's the wrong tool for the task.

Because finding and acknowledging our feelings are important to good mental health, the Daily Sharing Time is needed, with its emphasis on finding and sharing feelings every day in the safety of an intimate relationship. The Daily Sharing Time is quite simply good practice for growing self-awareness, rather like going to exercise class every day to keep muscles toned and fit.

The Daily Sharing Time is also important for the listener as well because these revealing moments help each person know of the moods and concerns of the other partner that are not easily recovered if they are missed for any reason. The Daily Sharing Time is a time of sharing feelings when we are not angry or frustrated. The Daily Sharing Time and the awareness it encourages then becomes an ally when disagreements occur.

All of us are motivated by a very complex network of feelings that lie within, rather like the many wires, cables, lines, and pipes that surprisingly lie under every city street. That inner network, which some scientists call pathways, influences our choices, from the clothes we buy to our behavior during a traffic gridlock.

And yet we seldom identify our feelings, even to ourselves, much less verbalize them to someone else. We may occasionally admit to being in "a bad mood," but the regular sharing of feelings with a trusted companion is not something we are accustomed to doing. Staying with a rational analysis of an issue is much safer and more profitable, we tell ourselves, as though only facts and opinions can be counted on, as if emotions are something untrustworthy and unreliable, not a factor in either decision-making or action.

Telling ourselves not to "be emotional" is much like telling ourselves not to have asthma or an ingrown toenail. Emotions may be inconvenient, but they are part of the psyche of all humans. All of us are going to have feelings about most issues, whether we want to acknowledge them or not. Processing our feelings leads to self-awareness. Processing our feelings can often lead to the resolution of a problem, which without that process is only partially understood.

When feelings are shared, it can lift the burden of carrying them inside the person who shares and bring relief. As for the partner, it can enrich with a clearer awareness of what has been a point of concern and sometimes even the engine that drives behavior concerning a specific issue. This special knowledge can provide the couple a way to deepen their understanding of each other and quite often will lead to a new appreciation.

Here is how David and Vera processed their feelings about money and made a decision about how they would handle financial issues in the future.

After Cambridge and during the time of a worldwide economic depression, David had gone to work in the London slums as part of a mission project of the United Methodist denomination. Seeing the abject poverty in the slums and responding to its needs with compassion, David often donated nearly all of his salary just to help others in their time of crisis. Giving away his money was not an issue to him, he said, because his habit was to spend as little as possible on himself. He felt confident that he could take care of himself since his needs were "meager."

Other than a hot cup of coffee and a book of coupons for bus rides, he said that he had no desire for anything else. He had no overcoat, Vera pointed out, until long after they were married. He wore an old raincoat that he had since college days and found no need for anything else, even though they lived in a cold climate. He either rode a bicycle from his adolescent years or used public transportation. He had no savings account nor did he want one. He had little thought about the future.

Also, David could not be bothered to keep records or to get receipts for what he did spend. He was quite content to live unencumbered by paper trails of expenses and payments. Money was not important to him, and thus, he believed that he needed no record of it.

Vera, on the other hand, was used to maintaining herself financially with a good job. "I never had much money," she said, "but I had enough to take care of myself and I knew how to do it." She had helped her father with household accounting when she was growing up, and as an independent woman, she said that she expected with those skills to be able when the time came for marriage "to take care of my own house."

Also, Vera kept "meticulous" records and always knew exactly where her money had gone. She felt financial solvency and stability were essential to any family, even though she thought that all families should live frugally and always within their means.

Then in 1933 David and Vera got married and were forced to face their very different habits and feelings about money. The euphoria of early marriage days lasted only a year or more, and then they were forced to confront their differences. David said that they "clashed head-on" (making the following an example of the step in the Anger Contract about expressing feelings). Vera preferred to remember that she merely expressed her feelings of distress about what she feared was going to happen to them if they did not make changes.

But it was their processing—taking their feelings seriously, especially Vera's since hers were stronger—that is helpful to couples today. Here is a model of expressing their feelings to each other and using their expressions to reach a decision about financial solvency for their future:

> *Vera:* I had several main objections about my new status as "wife." First of all, I felt bereft because, following the conventions and expectations of the day, I gave up my job when we married. I had been the Executive Director of a woman's organization for several years after college. I was responsible

for myself and my own money, traveled around Europe on my own, and felt confident about taking care of myself.

I did not know that part of my identity as a woman would go away with giving up that job and what it symbolized. I did not expect to feel that I had lost my way in the world.

Suddenly I had no money, and I was supposed to depend on my husband to support me. Fortunately, I had taken my annuities with me when I left my job, and I had put them into a savings account. This was the money that we later used to take our daughters to safety when WWII began.

The expectations at that time were that when a man gets married, he should be able to support his wife "in the manner to which she was accustomed," including a house. We did not have a house, only a tiny housing allowance, and David could provide nothing toward equipping our new apartment.

Fortunately, we had some wedding presents that helped with necessary furnishings, but we mostly did without the niceties and comforts. I was puzzled about this. I did not grow up in this kind of situation, and it had not been my environment as a young professional in the business world. Finally, I had to share with David the way I was feeling.

David: But before she shared this with me, I was already feeling bad about myself because I saw that I was not really as responsible as a married man should be. I shared my feelings with Vera about it, including that I wanted to change my pattern. I knew that in time a family would be coming and that I would have new responsibilities. It was a new status for me, too, and one that was showing me that my philosophy of money was entirely inappropriate. I just didn't know what to do about it.

Vera: I needed him to see that I was concerned about having no money personally. I expected us to live frugally. As the war loomed closer, there was even a slogan that advised all the

British to "Mend and make do." I was willing to abide by that advice and even felt patriotic about it, but I still yearned for some money of my own. I felt very strongly about this and said so.

Another objection as our marriage went along was that I felt hypocritical. David was supposed to provide me with money for housekeeping, and he did. But the convention of the day was that if a wife was smart enough, she would save a little money out of the housekeeping allowance and use that for herself. I felt that was rather a back-door kind of method and to do it made me feel like a hypocrite, even dishonest.

I wanted some money of my own, not an allowance. I wanted the money of my own for which I was in no way answerable. I wanted money to buy David a present, if I wanted to, or to buy myself a new book. I needed to be able to do it without asking someone else for permission.

David: Money is often a subject that brings out many strong feelings. In fact, we were once asked if we thought the practice of the husband managing the money was the right one, and I said, "Certainly not." I was remembering our early days and how disastrous for us it would have been if I had remained in charge of the funds. My attitudes toward money, including that I could not justify saving any when I saw other people's needs all around me, would have made grave difficulties for us.

Fortunately, in one of our early sessions of the sharing of feelings about the issue, I saw Vera's point of view and agreed to turn our financial affairs over to her. She would run the household and take charge of the bank account. She would do a much better job of that than I would, I clearly saw.

Vera: But it was not just managing well the money that David earned. I was willing to use my skills to make that salary go as far as possible. I even took pride in keeping us afloat. It was that I wanted the money of my own. It may have been the system for women at the time to make do on an "allowance," but I didn't like the system. I still don't.

Another concern was David's habit of giving money away to the indigent and supporting other people who did not have a job. Some of them really needed it as much as we did, but some of them turned out to be sociopaths and could not be helped no matter how much David gave them.

I feared that he did not realize what was involved in running a house and keeping a wife, that his pattern was established already on quite a different basis. I didn't want to change him from the generous person that he was that I loved, but I wanted him miraculously to see that he couldn't give his money away and also keep a home going.

David: I did come to see the reality of some of Vera's concerns, and I was in the process of adjusting some of my habits to fit those concerns when WWII intervened. It suddenly became necessary for her to take our girls across the Atlantic in 1940. But when she came back to England and we set up housekeeping again, it was clear that we had some of the same feelings and concerns about money as before. So, we tried once again to examine and share our feelings and ideas.

The first thing we learned as we examined our feelings was that there were some fundamental values we both shared. We were both brought up to believe that you didn't have a thing until you could pay for it, so we did not have a car until we could buy it outright. Fortunately for us, in the first post-war years, there were very few new cars available anyway in England, so that was not a problem. But we both shared this value and do to this day. Debt is just not something either of us is comfortable with.

The only situation in which we ever went into debt was in buying a house, and that was after we had moved to the US. I borrowed some money from my father to pay for the house, but I was very eager to pay it back as soon as possible. I paid off the whole debt in five years. We really deprived ourselves of many things during that time just to get that debt paid off.

The second thing we did as we examined our feelings about money was to take seriously Vera's feelings about needing some money of her own. As we both began to work for the Marriage Guidance Council, we divided the salaries each of us earned. We kept them separate and even divided the money from speaking engagements I had at the time. I hoped that this would deal with some of her early reluctance to live on an allowance as though she were a child. She got her part of all income; I got mine.

This decision was made before we moved to the US, but the outcome of our mutual understanding has continued to this day. The money that we divided now constitutes Vera's savings and my savings. We decided to have separate checking accounts and separate savings accounts. It was and is an arrangement that suits us exactly.

I pay the rent, the utilities, and the telephone charges. Vera pays all the household expenses, buys the groceries, and buys our clothes. Any extra expenses we discuss together and arrange which checking account it should come out of.

I saw clearly that this financial issue was really about more than money. I saw that it was to Vera a question of her personhood and identity. The salaries did not amount to much money, but taking her feelings seriously was an important step in re-establishing who she was in her own eyes.

Vera: It made me feel like a real partner in the marriage. To me, it was an element of trust. To deny a wife money of her own is to suggest that she is irresponsible. And the division of the money was very generous of David. But it was a proud day for me when I took out my first checking account under the name of Vera C. Mace.

David: That was just making up for all the time before that I didn't understand the importance to Vera of having money of her own. It took me a while, but I did learn to understand it.

Then the third thing we learned was that we both believed in frugality as a helpful habit. This was true long before the Depression and War Years. Also, we both believed in living beneath our income.

Vera: Yes, we determined that even when we had moved to the U.S and David was making money writing for the magazines, we would meet our total expenses and live on $10,000 a year. Anything above that we would put into savings. And we are still doing that; we have not diverged.

We educated our children on the yearly $10,000 and made all our travels around the world within that financial limit. Sometimes our way was paid by the people or governments who invited us, but sometimes it was not. We also went back to England once a year for twenty years to check on our families, and the money always came out of the $10,000.

David: But that is our service to others. It is not our own personal indulgence.

Then the fourth thing we learned—or more accurately had confirmed—was that I could never manage to keep good records of our expenditures, and Vera always had receipts and records. I still do not remember to write down what I spend money on even today because basically I was not and am not interested in it. Vera does a good job keeping track of our finances, and we are lucky that she is so diligent. Neither of us is likely to change. We depend on her for accurate records for taxes and business expenses.

To this day, Vera does not have to explain anything she chooses to do with her money. It is hers. And any check that now comes in for things we have both done or things we have both written, I simply divide in half. She deposits her half; I deposit mine.

Once I understood the strength and magnitude of Vera's feelings, it was an easy decision to make. I could not change the way I felt (and feel) about money, but that did not mean

Vera had to feel the same way. Nor did either of us have to be bound by the choices the other made. We simply settled the distribution of our money in a way that suited us both. No one had to change, but each personality and the feelings that are a part of the personality were honored. Processing the feelings allowed us to make an informed and practical decision.

Even our wills are separate, handled in a way that fits us still, after the initial decision to provide her with her own resources. Each of our daughters is provided for, of course, but we have also left small amounts of money to those relatives and friends who have mattered to us over the years. They all get something, but we do not make the same choices. And the money comes out of each of our savings accounts, which have been kept separately all these years. We do not decide on gifts or donations together, honoring Vera's strong feelings about making her own financial decisions.

Vera: None of our parents or relatives understood or agreed with the way we settled our financial situation. When David's mother was making her will, she thought she should leave the little she had to both her children. David finally convinced her that he did not need her money and his sister could really use it, but she only settled the issue by writing into her will that David wanted it this way.

All the extended family thought our decision on handling money went against social norms, and perhaps it did, but it fit for us and still does.

I never worry about money anymore, because we settled the issue long ago according to our feelings. Our decision was fair; it was equitable; it showed respect for both persons; it kept both of us feeling heard and understood; and it has kept our relationship uncluttered from financial concerns.

The Woods' Experience with Processing Feelings

One Saturday morning Bobbye decided to paint the outside French doors to the back porch as a surprise for Britton. To save money at the time of painting several rooms, Britton had decided not to include that door and to do the painting himself. Bobbye found the correct paint can in the garage, chose a clean paintbrush, and went to work on the doors, confident that it would be a good gift.

She was about halfway through when Britton came home from tennis, saw what she was doing, and angrily told her she should have used masking tape around the glass panes and put newspapers down on the floor of the porch to catch the drips. She should stop painting immediately, he said.

Bobbye was surprised by his verbal attack and criticism, since she was the one actually doing the work and it looked alright to her. She answered back in the same angry tone. They confronted each other toe to toe.

Since many years earlier they had made a mutual commitment to growth and through Marriage Enrichment had learned how to address their disagreements, they stopped a moment to examine what was happening, including processing the feelings which had been roused by the scene. This is what they discovered about motivation, anger, and guilt when they talked to each other about feelings:

Bobbye: *I felt sad* that you were not appreciative or happy that those doors were getting painted. *I was shocked* when you unfairly criticized me for doing a job that *I had expected* would be welcome. I had a mental picture of you coming home and being very pleased to find it done. *I felt stupid* to have tried to do something that you so obviously didn't want to be done.

Britton: You were doing it all wrong and *I didn't want* you to get paint on the glass panes or the cement.

Bobbye: I was being careful. *I was hurt* that you were so critical about a job I was doing for you.

Britton: I understand, and I can see how you felt. But, well, here is another part of the issue. *I felt embarrassed* that months ago I had said I would paint the door, and I never got around to it. I am not doing what I said I would do, and *I felt guilty* about it.

Bobbye: OK. I get that *I was hurt*, and *you were embarrassed*. We both reacted too quickly. But what are we going to do about the doors? One of them is still wet with paint.

Britton: I'll go get another paintbrush and work with you, and I'll bring some masking tape and newspapers for us both.

Bobbye: But I'm almost through with one door, and *I want to finish* it before we have lunch. Why don't you just fix the other door the way you want? I'll finish my door and bring us something cool to drink.

Britton: Okay.

The doors got painted, the anger soon subsided, and the Woods could laugh because at the end the doors looked about the same in quality of painting. But the time spent in processing feelings enlightened them both and created understanding even if they have different work styles (and probably always will). Verbalizing and processing the feelings kept the whole scene from becoming mired in unresolved issues or future resentment.

Couple Exercise

In this exercise, instead of finding the feeling and expressing it, think of an action your partner does that produces a certain feeling in you. Complete each of the following:

1. I feel appreciated when you …
2. I feel valued when you …
3. I feel understood when you …

Chapter 9

Openness and Intimacy

Apparently, a large section of the American population is so starved for intimate connections that lucrative businesses have proliferated offering warm, non-sexual hugs and touches for profit (e.g., Cuddle Up to Me, A Starbucks for Hugs) Those who frequent these businesses insist on both physical and emotional benefits: lowered blood pressure, increased attention, lessening and less severe episodes of depression, boosted immune system, more optimistic and positive outlook on life.

While the Maces endorsed the value of affectionate touches in close relationships, they were also convinced of a similar impact using words. They believed that sharing ourselves, openly and verbally, has a strong impact on the health and longevity of the relationship.

The sharing process—physical or verbal—leads to what a retiring President of the prestigious National Council on Family Relations once called "marriage enjoyment." He had looked at all the research measuring marital "success and happiness, satisfaction and adjustment," he said. He was proud of what the members of his organization now knew about the ways to be productive in a marriage relationship and the ways a stable and satisfying marriage could contribute worthwhile things to society.

What he really wanted to speak about in his farewell address (as his term of office expired) was what he referred to as "the goodies of the skin." This is seldom measured, he said, and seldom joyfully proclaimed, but it is what leads couples to security, adventure, laughing, sharing, comfort, and above all "marriage enjoyment." In addition to the special words of intimacy, couples need to speak to each other often, the retiring president wanted them to remember the specific value of touch and what it contributes to the partners' sense of well-being. Both provide the perfume of intimacy—friendship, ease, and peace.

Like jumper cables applied to a weak battery, honest words of self-disclosure—words not shared with others—have the power to ignite feelings of excitement and warmth badly needed by many weary lovers, tired from the daily round of meeting obligations and performing duties. Here is what the Maces said about openness and intimacy:

> ***Bobbye:*** One Marriage Enrichment term that you have used in talking about the Daily Sharing Time is "openness." And in many ways, we have already been talking about openness. But say some more about that.
>
> ***David:*** Until two people really know who they are, they cannot build a relationship. So, openness is like turning the light on and seeing the relationship clearly, as well as the two people in it. Openness can begin at any time in the relationship, but it needs to be carefully defined.
>
> When we talk about openness, we are talking about being open to each other, being willing to share information about ourselves, our likes and dislikes, our future hopes, our secret fears, our daily celebrations and concerns. This is the level of access to real intimacy for a couple.

Britton: When you talk about openness, are you also talking about honesty?

David: Yes, certainly that is a part of it. But the final ethic in relationships is not the ethics of honesty but the ethics of love. *The ethic of honesty can become brutal frankness when it violates the ethics of love.*

Bobbye: I remember something you wrote that said that the ethics of honesty was not the highest in a couple relationship—if all it does is relieve the speaker's mind.

David: Yes, in long years of counseling I encountered so many of these situations which were so disruptive to the relationship. I saw again and again that the ethics of honesty was not the highest ethics. Simply to spill everything out without regard to what it's going to do to your partner can be a very unloving act.

Britton: So, openness is the freedom to share fully—and the freedom not to share, if it cannot be done through the ethics of love.

David: Yes, but you must not merely hide behind a handy motivation that you are avoiding honesty because it may hurt the other person. What I say is that there are at least three guidelines for avoiding complete honesty with your partner:

1. The first is when you are the recipient of a confidence from someone else, someone whom you told you would keep their confidence.
2. The second is when you have a very negative feeling against your partner which could be spilled out in a thoughtless way at an inopportune moment and could hurt deeply. You are not free to spill out your negative feelings without consideration of what they will do.
3. And the third is where a confession would deeply disturb and shock your partner. It's ideal, of course, to share everything, but you don't have the right to get peace of mind for

> yourself at the expense of deeply hurting your partner. But if it is something that affects you and is constantly on your mind, you should spit it out to someone else like a counselor or a trusted friend. And if at a later date the partner does discover the indiscretion or whatever it is, you can always refer them to the counselor or friend so that the partner knows you did not tell them about it out of consideration for them.

Vera: It's like a function of confession in the Catholic Church?

David: Yes, it is except that the friend or counselor does not have the authority to absolve you of your indiscretion just because you confessed it.

Bobbye: So, honesty is a component of the openness concept, but honesty is to be tempered by love.

David: Yes, the ethics of honesty is subservient. But what we are talking about is the extreme outer frontiers of relationship. What we are really interested in is the day-to-day continuing openness to each other in our thoughts, interests, intentions, wishes, desires. Because our feelings really represent us as we are; *if we don't share our feelings, we don't share ourselves.*

Britton: What if a person is reluctant to share feelings or to be open to the partner? How can he or she move to a position of openness?

David: Marriage Encounter has a very helpful exercise called the 10 and 10. It means that a couple takes ten minutes to write down some thoughts and feelings about themselves, the partner, and the relationship. Then later in the day for another ten minutes the partners read what each other has written. They read it once "with the head" and once "with the heart." Then they share anything they want to say to each other. This is how Marriage Encounter gets couples into the practice of talking to each other about feelings.

Marriage Encounter deals with this issue in a very successful way, I think. The written list becomes a bridge that gives a little distance, just enough to make it comfortable to do. The couples often find this a breakthrough in the communication of something very personal, like feelings.

Vera and I do a similar thing and it has come to be called by Marriage Enrichment the Daily Sharing Time. I make us a cup of tea, bring it to Vera in bed as we start the morning, and we share our hopes and expectations for the day. We also share the feelings that we are having about ourselves and about each other.

It is useful to me to know, for example, where Vera is in her feelings because I can see there are some things I do not need to say at that time. If she is down, for example, I will just hold some of them for a better time. It helps me to know her feelings but also the intensity of those feelings.

Sharing feelings is an important part of developing intimacy, and *intimacy is what couples need, especially if they are very busy,* their schedules are crowded, and time together is hard to find.

Bobbye: Suppose one partner is becoming increasingly willing to share and perhaps even begins to desire this new level of intimacy or a more open level of communication, and the other partner is becoming defensive and obviously scared to do it? Are there some ways that the reluctant partner can become more open?

David: The psychology of self-disclosure is what helps us here. Psychology is finding that all deep friendships are based on self-disclosure. Most people have felt that it is common interests that deepen friendships. Common interests merely bring people together, but it is mutual self-disclosure that produces depth in friendships. But self-disclosure must be phased, and it must be balanced. For instance, if one person discloses in one big bang, it could have a negative effect. There must be small moments of self-disclosure rather than one violent moment.

With couples, the Daily Sharing Time, a conversation that includes one's feelings at the moment, is a very helpful process in making both partners comfortable. The daily dialogue becomes a process. What you can say today may not be what you can say tomorrow as trust increases and self-disclosure becomes easier.

The ability to be vulnerable is a skill that is learned only by increments and cannot be forced. In fact, it may not be good for a person to spill everything out at once. There is a question of the value of too-much-too-soon. A steady and deepening sharing gives both partners' confidence and allows both to develop skills of listening, as well as sharing.

What I am doing is trying to answer your question about one partner being willing to share and the other not. Perhaps the reluctant partner is right and too much openness too soon can be detrimental to the relationship. So, to set up a daily conversation is a way to gently experiment with how to be a little more open. Doing it gradually over time helps both persons to feel comfortable with the process.

This is an important tenet of self-disclosure: It must be gradually phased over time. *Trust cannot be established by force.* Disclosing oneself gradually helps both partners feel more comfortable, and it also allows each partner time to become aware of feelings. Some people take longer than others to discover what they really feel.

The Oriental custom is helpful here of the Chinese merchant. He wants to sell you something, but he begins by asking how you are, who is in your family, where you live, and general questions about your life. Then he tells you something about himself and his family. This is used as a method of beginning a transaction by discovering areas of commonality.

Only in due course does the merchant workaround to the proposition of a commercial exchange that both merchant and customer knew was coming. But it is done in a polite and simple way and relaxes whatever exchange is to follow. It takes a while, but it is the preferred process in the Oriental world. It does not force the issue, and many couples could profit from a soft and friendly approach to self-disclosure.

Bobbye: I once read a story about a woman whose husband tells her in the restaurant where they are having dinner that on his latest business trip to New York he has met another woman and has fallen in love with her. She jumps to her feet in alarm. He stands before her and says he never intended this to happen.

He weeps, asks for her forgiveness, tells her he will be leaving her, and gives her the name of the lawyer he will be using. He lists the things they both need to do regarding their business for the future. He asks her not to think harshly of him and suggests what might be an easy method for telling friends and family about their reasons for divorce. He asks for her understanding.

It is just too much for her all at once, and she rushes frantically out of the restaurant. She finally walks over to a trash barrel on the sidewalk and throws up, because she is so powerfully moved both by his sudden news and by his suddenly voiced expectations of what she will and will not do. This couple episode is NOT what you mean when you talk about openness and self-disclosure.

David: Indeed not. There are graduations in every relationship, and that is especially true of the marriage relationship. Not everyone desires the same amount of openness, and everyone has very different reasons for wanting it or not wanting it. These reasons are important and can only be revealed over time as the person examines his or her own feelings and

THEN decides to disclose or not disclose. Rushing into a premature disclosure can make it hard to ever get back to trust and openness. The slow but steady process of disclosure is imperative.

The feelings are a part of the person and must be acknowledged and examined. Both partners have to know themselves and know each other. This is the way that openness and intimacy are established. But the process needs to proceed at a level of comfort for both.

Britton: What if a couple has not progressed to the level that you two have concerning shared feelings? How can a couple decide to move deeper in this? Is it strictly through the practice? Are there some steps toward fuller expression? Is there a process?

David: There often must be a point when a couple sees this is something they have to do. It might come after a conflict, but something happens that makes them realize that they must open up their feelings. Sometimes they have to go through a painful initial experience of clearing all the negative and hurtful stuff out.

Then when that has been done, it is a matter of sustaining the relationship and the good feelings produced by dealing with the troublesome issues in this way. It is a process, as you say, but one that can lead to real intimacy once the issues and the feelings surrounding them have been aired and expressed.

Vera: But sometimes I don't know right away what my feelings are.

Britton: Neither do I. There are times when I have been unable to focus on my feelings and to verbalize them.

David: I often recommend to people a very simple exercise. I went through long periods of depression when I was a teenager. This is what I did then and what I recommend to this day:

1. Get a sheet of paper and write down what your feelings are. Make a list.
2. Then try to assign a reason as to why you might have any of those feelings. Was it something that happened yesterday? Something you read? If possible, find the causes for the feelings on your list.
3. Then look at these causes and see if there is any specific action you can take. If there is, go and do it.

This is an easy way of learning to be in touch with your feelings. It is done privately, and then when the person is comfortable with what he is finding, he or she can more easily share with the partner.

Britton: I talked to a lady recently who was very pleased with her life. She was pleased with her work situation, with her home life, and with her two children. Yet she would end every day crying. She was unable to figure it out. She said that she couldn't think of anything that would make her sad, but still she cried uncontrollably every evening.

My suggestion to her was that something in her subconscious mind was troubling her and that it was affecting her at the emotional level, causing her to cry. Whatever it was had not yet reached the conscious level of understanding. I told her that I thought she would eventually figure it out. But I wish that I had known about this list.

David: Yes, our subconscious mind often lets us know important things about ourselves. The list is just one way of trying to understand it.

Britton: Do you believe in the importance of dreams?

David: Up to a point. I think dreams can help us get hold of and be aware of the complex crises of our lives.

Britton: Do you write them down when you wake up?

David: Sometimes, but I usually just tell them to Vera. I don't mean I tell her every single dream I have. But if it is a disturbing dream, I tell her. In telling her, I am also telling myself. Sometimes a bad or a negative dream is just our subconscious trying to get our attention.

Britton: Do you tell Vera about your bad dreams as a part of your Daily Sharing Time?

David: Yes.

Vera: And David remembers his dreams much better than I do. But what this conversation is opening up for me is the subject of refusing to recognize our feelings. I think we need to give ourselves permission to have, to recognize, and to share our feelings.

David: Sometimes the subconscious is trying to tell us something—even in dreams—and I am refusing to own what is happening. You, Vera, say you do not dream very often. Perhaps that makes you a much more complicated person than I am. You deal with your feelings at the conscious level. You are rarely out of touch with your deepest self.

I have more trouble doing that, so I have dreams that try to get my attention so that I can address them at a more analytical level. When I was growing up, for example, I at first tried to block out all the depressing thoughts I was having, and I had very powerful dreams.

Another time was when I was having trouble deciding whether to be a minister or not; another was when I had a series of heart attacks and lived in a twilight state for a while. Keeping a record of my feelings and dreams during those times was a way of getting in touch with what was happening to me and beginning to make decisions concerning what I could do about it.

Bobbye: When I was finishing up my graduate degree, I went through a period of consciously not acknowledging my feelings. It was a difficult period and one that was very tightly packed with decisions and tasks. We were raising three daughters and two were teenagers. I was teaching at two different universities while I was also writing my dissertation.

I thought I could not deal with my feelings, and I knew I had to keep going. I feared that if I cried or gave any indication of how awful things felt to me, I could not even continue functioning. I simply ignored all my emotions and concentrated on my tasks.

I went so long without acknowledging my feelings, that once the crisis period had passed and I had graduated, I had no way to be proud of what I had accomplished and no way to enjoy the outcome of an advanced degree. I had erased every feeling of any kind when I failed to acknowledge the strong negative feelings I was having. I had not gone through the graduation ceremony and I had not been hooded. My family had no celebrations with me.

David: The fact that you could do that without some kind of breakdown shows your inner strength, though. Perhaps some of your feelings were expressed in the dreams you had at that time. It would be interesting if you could have probed them to find out what they were trying to tell you.

Bobbye: Possibly, I would like to feel better about that time in my life, but I seem to have lost the bridge to go back and examine it.

David: Many of my dreams now are about end-of-life issues. When we founded Marriage Enrichment, we began with great hopes for what might happen although it was slow. Then within a ten-year period, everything began to accelerate and expand beyond our greatest dreams. All around the world MEGs were formed, speaking engagements proliferated, organizations invited us to publish with them, and many books got written. We received multiple awards in recognition of what we had begun many years earlier in war-time England.

Now that all these things are established, we will soon not be around to enjoy them. It seems such a shame, and I am in a state of inward rebellion against the awareness that life is growing to a close.

Already I find that my ability to remember names is declining. But the thing I dread most is the possibility that my mind will cease to function effectively. That really weighs on me very heavily. These concerns are those come up in my dreams at the present time. It is the awareness that my life is nearly over, and I don't like that. I had shared this fact of life with my medical students in purely an academic way, but now that it is a fact that I must leave this beautiful world and all the pleasant people in it, I rail against the fact.

Bobbye: And when you have a dream about ending your career that seems to be about all your underlying fears and uncertainties, naturally you would want to get in touch with it.

David: Yes, that's exactly where I am. And Vera understands this, you see. It is comforting to me to know that someone so close to me understands how I feel. I have exceeded the life-expectancy time given by the doctor after my heart attacks—one of them quite severe—and I am grateful for exceeding the time predicted for me. But something inside just won't accept the facts. Something persists in saying it is not fair.

Bobbye: You said about the Marriage Encounter procedure with the exercise that they call the 10 and 10 that a person reads the feeling list once with "the head" and once with "the heart." On this subject, your head tells you that you are lucky to have exceeded a certain predicted time period, but your heart still objects.

Vera: I don't think my feelings about growing old are the same as David's. I feel sad that I've left so many things undone and someone else will have to clear up all my unfinished business. I have pieces of embroidery that I have left undone, and I badly need to clean out my kitchen cabinets so that someone else will not have to do it. There are no relatives around to help. One daughter lives here in the US, but she is several states away. Our other daughter lives in Spain. All the other relatives live in England. My feelings about that issue do not come out in dreams, however.

Bobbye: Let's talk about identifying and articulating feelings, whether or not they express themselves in dreams. That's where we began, and it's such an important point regarding intimacy that I would like to get back to that. What are some ways that a person can start when he hasn't had much practice in this?

David: Writing down one's feelings in order to identify them, as I said earlier, is a good place to start. Writing down feelings is a prelude to being able to speak them aloud. *But it's the sharing feelings with one's partner that leads to healing and builds trust.* Sharing the feelings gives you the sense of being known and understood.

It releases you from your sense of isolation. It's good to know what your feelings are, but if you are alone with them, you may feel even more cut off. *Sharing those feelings with someone who loves you and is trying to understand you may be one of the most important benefits that marriage provides.*

Bobbye: What if the feelings are negative, even negative toward the husband or wife? What if the sharing produces hostility in the other person?

David: That doesn't make any difference. All our work has shown the benefits of a productive way to deal with anger. Our work in the field of conflict resolution has helped us to give each other full permission to be angry, even to be angry with each other. Working the anger process through, going through all the steps, gives each of us a new understanding of what has happened and how we feel about it. It also frequently shows us a way to act in order to avoid a similar confrontation again.

You might say there are three stages in processing the journey from anger to resolution:

1. The first stage is being aware of your own feelings. You can accomplish this awareness best by writing down the feelings and analyzing them.
2. The second stage is sharing those feelings with a trusted partner and thereby escaping from the isolation of being trapped in your own feelings.
3. The third stage is using the interpersonal feelings that belong to the marriage to grow the relationship.

This third stage is where the greatest growth occurs, as you begin to clear up the issues expressed in the negative or angry feelings. *When you have a way to process and diffuse the angry feelings that come to everyone, you have taken an important step toward growth and couple intimacy.*

Vera: About writing down feelings: I think you have to assume that we are talking about a person who ordinarily does this as a way to understand feelings during an angry period. Anger is such a volatile emotion that some people would not automatically pick up a pen and write. A person of little education might find it impossible to do. What about them?

David: Anger is a secondary emotion. You have to find the primary emotion under it and deal with it. Anger is almost a classical instance of the value of this process for dealing with it productively.

We assume that people who have quick flashpoints of angry feelings, or people of little education, cannot do it.

But after long years of getting letters from all kinds of people when I was writing columns, I reached the conclusion that the degree of education is not of any consequence. When the feeling is high, most people can find the language to express their feelings, sometimes very vividly. Uneducated people may be closer to their feelings; they don't build up these complicated networks of pretenses and defenses.

Sometimes in the days when I was publishing my newspaper and magazine columns, I got letters badly misspelled and poorly punctuated but very clear in expressing what the writer thought and felt. On the contrary, sometimes the educated person just wrapped everything up in innuendoes, and it was impossible to tell what they felt and even what question they wanted to be answered. I don't think one's economic status has much to do with one's expression of feelings and wishes.

People who lose their temper quickly and easily can also learn to use this process with great success. The important thing is getting in touch with your feelings and learning to share them with the people you care about. Often a flash of anger is just the time to push us to employ something different, something we have not used before.

The point is we cannot withhold this vital part of ourselves and at the same time have closeness and intimacy with our life partners. We cannot hope to succeed if we do not openly share ourselves with each other. We cannot leave the partner to guess or to assume what is going on within us.

Personal words about ourselves, our feelings and our aspirations, our needs and concerns, our past and our hope for the future, have a profound effect. Sharing ourselves in this way establishes a bond between partners. It moves the relationship to a deeper level.

A recent *Time* magazine article reports about a growing body of research recounting the benefits of better health when there are warm and open interactions between married partners. Some of the research studies examined show better health when there are frequent intimate exchanges; some show partners who feel so valued by intimate exchanges that they are "much more likely to exercise" and to eat healthily. One study even recounts "fewer depressive symptoms" and less stress. Under a heading called "Spousal Interactions can have BIG Benefits," these words appear:

> *Having a thoughtful conversation with a spouse can not only increase intimacy but also improve health in meaningful and lasting ways. A study of 162 married or cohabiting couples found that on days when they had a pleasant, positive conversation, the partners felt less lonely and more intimate, and fell asleep faster, than on days when they didn't. Interactions in our relationships impact us more than we think.*

Apparently, this substantial body of research, along with the popular Cuddle.com, provides both physical and emotional evidence of the benefits of touch and of sweet, personal, and intimate words.

The Woods' Experience with Openness and Intimacy

One day at their daily couple time, Britton and Bobbye wrote in their answers completing the following sentences. Then they shared their answers and explained why they responded as they did. It led to a sweet couple time, as two people endeavored to let each other know their opinions, memories, and feelings:

1. **I was attracted to you mainly because of your ...**
   Bobbye: From our very first meeting, I noticed your sense of humor. I have always liked it. Also, I was attracted by the ideals that I saw both of us shared.

Britton: I was attracted to your happy spirit and interest in singing, an interest that both of us had.

2. **Our marriage has survived because ...**
Bobbye: We intended from the beginning that our marriage would last, and we tried to do the things that would keep it strong.

Britton: We both have put the work in. We want it. We choose it.

3. **One thing I've learned to accept about you is ...**
Bobbye: You are going to talk straight about what is on your mind. You can be polite about it and ask, "Is this a good time to talk?" But you are going to address issues that need to be talked about. I count on that.

Britton: You want acceptance and full disclosure, and you want it to be genuine.

4. **To me a delightful surprise in our marriage has been ...**
Bobbye: A big surprise was that in our sixtieth year together we made a new connection that has led to closeness and a new sense of playfulness and fun. I thought we had experienced everything already, and I am so happy to learn that marriage can be an ever-developing process.

Britton: I agree. But it was a surprise to me when we married that you didn't know how to cook. The one meal that I thought you had prepared when we were dating was actually cooked by your aunt. Then when we came back from our honeymoon, I learned the true facts. But I am happy that you have become an excellent cook. You are certainly much more than that.

5. **If we could throw caution to the wind, I would like to ...**
Bobbye: I would like to go on a river cruise in Europe, one that goes all the way from Eastern Europe to Scandinavia.

Britton: I would like to do what we are doing right now. I am content.

Couple Exercise

(Share this exercise with your partner)

1. I was attracted to you mainly because of your …
2. Our marriage has survived because ,…
3. One thing I've learned to accept about you is …
4. To me a delightful surprise in our marriage has been …
5. If we could throw caution to the wind, I would like to …

Chapter 10
Group Dialogues and MEGs

The Maces were convinced that small group work was invaluable to couples who were committed to growth. Therefore, wherever they went in the world, they established groups of couples who agreed to meet for a specific period of time to share their experiences—never advice or opinions—and to be open to learn from each other.

Many of those MEGs can still be found, with even some second-generation couples attending. The Woods have participated in their MEG for over thirty-five years. In addition, they have attended MEG meetings in Maine, Missouri, Virginia, North and South Carolina, West Virginia, New Mexico, Kansas, California, Texas, and Florida, as well as in Australia, Mexico, Taiwan, and England.

The goals of the MEGs are simple:

- Help couples develop healthy ways of talking and listening to each other.
- Give couples needed support by building friendships with other couples who also are committed to growing a healthy relationship.
- Provide a safe environment for self-disclosure with the partner.
- Address subjects of interest to all couples by means of skill-building couple exercises.
- Design a couple growth experience that is also fun.

From their extensive experience with groups, the Maces believed firmly in the power of couple dialogue. David even called it "redemptive" when referring to what happened to groups listening to an authentic couple dealing with their couple issues. In fact, in their earliest groups the agenda for the meetings was built strictly around dialogue. *MEGs have changed in structure and emphasis over the decades, but the belief in the power of couple dialogue has not.* The couple dialogue is still the heart and soul of the MEG. Here are excerpts of the Maces' views on what group participation does both for the individual couple and for the group itself:

> ***David:*** There are several different types of dialogue, and all are useful to couples. The *Private Dialogue* is only for the couple itself to get an understanding of each other. The couple is talking back and forth with each other about their own issues and feelings. It is important, but it has no relevance to anybody else but the couple itself. It is usually referred to as the Daily Sharing Time and is meant for a couple to deepen their own relationship.
>
> However, as we observed the couple growth that the Daily Sharing Time provided so many couples we knew, we considered how it could be used in a group. With a bit of preparation about group process and communication techniques, couples could also talk to each other IN THE PRESENCE OF THE GROUP, talk to each other while they also allow other couples to listen.
>
> There is a strong power in an authentic dialogue done in the presence of a group that also wants good things for their own relationship. It may feel awkward the first time it is done but it also is a captivating experience.
>
> At its simplest level, the couple dialogue done in the presence of a group can merely be an exchange of observations and reflections on marriage. That is why we call it the *Reporting Dialogue.* A couple faces each other as they are a part of a group and reviews for each other the way that they have come.

This helps the group see the unique paths that couples have taken, as well as the issues those paths have brought forth. It is like narrating significant events, usually asking, "Do you remember?" It is comfortable and very nice, but there is no depth about it and very little feeling attached to it. We ask couples to take time with their reflections, considering responses to each other's memories and avoiding rushing into any conversation.

Vera: Yes, we also ask the group to be patient and not to feel that the couple must hurry through their reflections and their importance.

David: We also try to persuade the group not to interrupt, even by laughing. A couple dialoguing for the first time have to detach themselves from the group as an audience. The dialogue in the presence of others can be a scary thing for couples at first, and if the group keeps interrupting, this only intensifies the fact that their conversation is being done in public.

So, we ask the other couples not to intervene and not to ask questions. It can throw some dialoguing couples out of balance, even when they are enjoying their reflections, if they suddenly realize that they are not alone because someone laughs or intrudes with a comment. In fact, the social norm at this point would be to turn away from the partner and address the person who has said something to you. If that happens, it breaks the rhythm of the reporting dialogue, so we ask the group not to be intrusive.

Britton: But the group can have tremendous empathy as well. They are often very much on the side of the dialoguing couples.

David: Yes, even the Reporting Dialogue can exert a definite power. But for couples doing it for the first time, the group can be intimidating. When it is over, the reporting couple can ask for feedback or not. If they do, the appropriate response is not analysis or criticism but an underscoring of something they said, something that struck a responsive note on the part of the person giving feedback. The great thing is for everyone in the group to feel relaxed and comfortable, including the couple doing the Reporting Dialogue.

Bobbye: What is the second kind of dialogue?

David: Another kind of dialogue has the couple discussing an obstacle or issue which they have not yet resolved but want to. They may be actually and actively struggling with that issue in the presence of the group. This is called a *Working Dialogue,* where a couple is really working on an obstacle right there.

Sometimes it is so powerful that another couple is encouraged to say when they are finished, "We are there too. We are working on that same obstacle." Most couples do not know that other couples deal with the very same issues, and age and length of the relationship have very little to do it. But since in our society there is no forum to deal with this fact, most couples simply struggle on with little or no help. If it gets bad enough, they may confide in a friend or go to counseling, but sadly there is little knowledge that other couples face the same obstacles.

Working Dialogues touch the group as it sees the resources another couple is trying to use. It is a level of realism, an authentic voice of reality that is difficult to fake. As with the Reporting Dialogue, there is no advice given, no analysis, only a response to what they said that touches or instructs.

Bobbye: The first Marriage Enrichment retreat we attended was our first exposure to this concept. At first, I was hesitant to attempt a Working Dialogue in public, but as we progressed, I became aware of how much easier it was because of the support of the group. We were working on an issue that had already happened, so at first, our conversation didn't have the emotional impact of something that was immediately at hand that had not been processed.

It was concerning a holiday meal which I ended up preparing all by myself, even though there were other female relatives who were visiting and who might conceivably have helped in the preparation.

Only Britton was at home, and he was busy with a football game on TV and occasionally called into the kitchen where I was working making comments on what I was missing. It was the most exciting game he had seen in years, he reported, leaving me to feel sorry for myself with no help for a New Year's Eve dinner.

When everyone returned from a shopping trip (including our three teenaged daughters) and we finally sat down to eat, Britton found that he had no water in his glass, which was supposed to be a kind of passive/aggressive hint that I was not happy.

Even though the episode was a few weeks past, as we talked about that holiday meal, I found myself really getting into it—

Vera: You found that it was something not yet resolved?

Bobbye: Yes. And I remember as Britton and I started to talk about our family issue and its impact on our relationship, the group's circle of chairs was a good distance from us. As we discussed our options about what we as a couple could do if this ever happened again, although we were not talking softly, I became aware that the group was moving their chairs closer to us.

At one point in defining what I felt when neither my mother nor Britton's mother or sister offered any assistance, I asked Britton what I should have done. He replied that I could have stopped cooking. "What about the family?" I asked, and a gentleman in the group whom I had barely met stood up and said, "Pee on the family!"

I saw that as we had talked, the subject had struck a responsive chord with the group and many people had definite opinions about that issue and others like it because they had experienced something similar.

It had become an example of an empathetic group taking what apparently was a common issue of dealing with broader family occasions and coming down decidedly on the side of the couple. I still remember how surprised and how supported I felt. The solutions we came to quickly about what we would do regarding other holiday meals did not seem as important to me as the group encouragement and empathy.

Britton: Yes, and I remember the spontaneous laughter when this happened. There may even have been applause. It was a good example of how a group and a couple dialogue could interact when the topic is relevant to what couples really struggle with.

Bobbye: So, we have the Recording Dialogue, simple and reflective, and we have the Working Dialogue, which is to work through an issue or obstacle for a particular couple. Is there any other kind of dialogue?

David: Yes, we have the *Performing Dialogue*. This one is usually done by one couple in front of a large group or a specific audience. Its subject might be, for example, affirmation. It would be largely the same in structure as the other two—a back and forth speaking and response—but the speaker would have a longer time to say all the affirming things he wants to, without interruption or response. Then it would be the turn of the other person.

It is a dialogue because each person is going back and forth, taking turns. They are standing facing each other, unlike the knee-to-knee position of the other forms of dialogue. Each person just speaks for a longer time than in the other two.

Bobbye: Is there any other kind of dialogue?

David: Yes, there is one more, the *Witnessing Dialogue*. This one is very similar to the reporting dialogue and has several features that are the same. It is always public. It is where the couple shows their marriage so that others will know where they are currently and what issues specifically have brought them to their current position. It is not just narrating the marriage like the Reporting Dialogue; it is not merely describing it. It is not working on an issue, concentrating only on that subject. This style is demonstrating the marriage. It has a great impact.

Britton: How did you come to these different forms or styles of dialogue?

David: We were developing couple exercises for a training session we had been invited to do. We remembered a process called a dialogue that we had once witnessed at a Quaker meeting. One couple sat in the center of a circle and talked to each other. There were many pauses for reflection, which is in keeping with Quaker tradition. We discussed the process together, dropped the reflective pauses as cumbersome and awkward, kept the couple in the circle to avoid the difficulty of moving and rearranging chairs, and the Marriage Enrichment concept of the public couple dialogue was born.

We saw it in a new way to make a couple group function. In other words, *we found a way in which the marriage could speak.*

Britton: What about a couple who chooses not to dialogue in the group, for whatever reason? Do you have some suggestions for them?

David: We have various ways of dealing with couples who have difficulty dialoguing. One way is to have the couple discuss with each other about their feelings, what emotions they are experiencing and what concerns they have about the experience.

Another suggestion is made to couples apprehensive that something will be revealed during the dialogue that they are not ready to share in the group. We frequently ask that that couple first have a private conversation, to see if there is something that should not be said publicly that they can both agree to.

For those who are concerned about the way either of them might handle strong emotions or who are fearful that one partner might cry during the dialogue, we try to tell them that tears are just a way to show how deep feelings can be about certain subjects. We tell them that they are really honoring the group when they let the group see their deep feelings.

Another suggestion for a reluctant couple is to allow them some private time to discuss with each other about why that subject is too heavy or too personal to dialogue about in front of the group. We would proceed on the principle that you always focus on where you are now.

What you are doing is showing people that you need to take the logical step in front of you and not try to jump two steps ahead. Start with all anxious couples where they are, not where they have been or where they might want to be. In the free-flowing dialogue, it is important to keep the focus on the present.

Vera: Dialogue at its best is not a highly structured technique. Its power lies partly in its personal and easy-going style, and to put it into a formula of some kind may actually take away some of its power and give it a limitation. I like the liberty of a couple to say what is on their hearts, and I do not want to make it some kind of binding formula. I do not want it to be bound by a methodology.

If you commit yourself to the dialogue, you don't always know where it is going to take you or what is going to happen. This can be scary, but it also can be an authentic voice that touches people's hearts.

David: Yes, it isn't a streetcar track; it is an open road. It is not a performance made from a script; it is two people speaking to each other honestly and sincerely. And the spontaneity is both part of its charm and part of its unique power.

The Maces used the word "concerns" in the context of their group work. They were interested in how to get a diverse and somewhat apprehensive group to relax and work with each other.

But that context of arranging a group's comfort level is only on the surface. Underneath the surface is an important reminder to couples and families that their needs and concerns must be both communicated and honored. It is important that a person "own" his or her thoughts and feelings, and that he or she states those feelings openly in the safety of a supportive group.

When the concerns are communicated, it is an important moment that needs to be listened to and addressed by those to whom they are stated. Then the group or the family feels safe and whole; then the group or the family can trust each other, knowing that needs and concerns will be taken seriously by those who matter.

Here is what the Maces say about concerns:

Vera: We believe that bringing up a concern in a group should take priority over whatever else we are doing.

Britton: Is this just unique to Marriage Enrichment meetings or is this something you think couples need to deal with in their own relationship?

David: It is both. We say at the beginning that what we are going to deal with in the group are the things that couples want to deal with. Here's what we are trying to do: *we are trying to run the group the way the couples should run their marriages. When something is of concern to one person, it should take priority over other subjects.*

Britton: How did you come to this?

David: We discovered very early in our Marriage Enrichment meetings that the vital thing was for everybody in the group to feel really comfortable. If someone in the group was not comfortable, the group would not be able to function as well as it should. In analyzing after it was all over in some of our early groups, we discovered that sometimes one person was uncomfortable and not relaxed. It had inhibited the whole group.

Vera: Yes, they were present, you see, but they were not really present because they were worried or anxious about something. They were not comfortable within themselves or they were not comfortable in the group, and therefore they isolated themselves.

David: And we realized that this was damaging to the group and its fellowship, when someone had so isolated themselves. It was vital for the functioning of the group that everyone is relaxed.

So, in the interests of a developing group, we state at the beginning that someone should have the freedom to voice a concern. We felt that anything anyone was uncomfortable about should be shared, dealt with, and if possible, cleared up before we moved on. This was true for us as well as for anyone else in the group.

This has repeatedly proved its value. It may be that when people get together for any reason, half of them are not even there in their spirits because they are thinking about something else. We want people to be together and really involved. So, toward this end, we put people in circles, looking at each other. If you put them in rows, it is easy for some to put the correct expression on their faces and then think about whatever they want.

It is stating the rules about concerns that help people relax. We've had them tell us again and again that the freedom to express concerns in the group helps them all relax and feel comfortable together.

Bobbye: Suppose you encounter someone who expresses concerns often?

David: It doesn't matter. We will accept them.

Bobbye: Even if some other people in the group get bored or suspicious?

David: I don't think people ever get bored with hearing other's concerns. It says to them that we are sincere about the comfort level and they like it.

Vera: Perhaps we should say that a concern is only about an immediate situation. It is not about something that you brought with you and that is not relevant to the group.

David: Yes, we often have to ask for a rephrasing of the concern. We ask, "What is your concern? What exactly are you feeling now?" If it is something that has already happened in the past, we are not going to be able to deal with it.

Britton: You have said that the idea of concerns is part of your Quaker style. It also seems to me that oneness is part of your Quaker style.

David: We would like to encourage oneness in the spirit in our groups, and this is very much part of the Quaker style. We would like the group to feel that we are all in this project of couple growth together and we are all in fellowship together. We are all helping each other and supporting each other.

Vera: Another factor here is that when a concern is expressed to the group, it is the group that takes responsibility for an answer to the stated concern. It is not the leader who has to do something about it; it's the total group. That is a helpful philosophy for families, as well. The group helps take care of the group. There is no one autocratic leader who is expected to deal with any issue that troubles the group.

David: Yes, often when a concern is expressed, we will say to the group, "Now, what are we going to do about this?" We think a group should take responsibility for itself. We are not leaders in any authoritarian sense. We are merely participating facilitators.

Britton: You said that a concern expressed in a group was always a priority. Is that true in your relationship also?

David: Yes, everything else goes out the window until we can deal with the concern that one of us has. If you do not have this arrangement, you may foul things up.

Britton: It's just a method of communicating?

Bobbye: That's what it sounds like, but there is also the assurance that both persons are going to work on the concern. It is not just a worry for one person. If it is a concern for one person, it belongs to the relationship.

David: But Vera might be expressing a concern to me and if I were at that moment really involved in something else, it would be alright for me to say, "I don't see how we can work on that right now. Would it be ok to postpone that for the present?" But we both have the clearest understanding that we will get to it as soon as possible. Without that understanding, it would sound like we are not interested in the other person's issue.

The same could be said of a family. It is a guarantee that if you have a need, you are going to be heard. And that the other people want to hear from you. It is not an intrusion. Concerns and the expression of the concerns are important, simply because the group will not function as a group if the fellowship is broken. When concerns and specific statements of needs are expressed and dealt with, the group once again begins to function as a unit.

Groups, like couples and families, can only be helped in the context of where they are existential. You cannot help them where they may someday be. You cannot help undo what has already happened. You can only take them where they are and deal with that. And that involves the clear statement of the needs and concerns of the moment.

It is important for the person stating the concern to be clear and concise; that is a helpful lesson to learn. It is important for those listening, whether groups, couple, or family, to learn how to listen and respond to others. It is a communication growth technique.

Stating concerns involves others. Taking concerns seriously enough to respond sets a tone of acceptance and comfort for all those present. Someone cares, it says; someone is interested. I am safe. I am OK. This is true for groups; it is true for families; it is true for couples.

A MEG usually meets once a month for the duration of an agreed-upon time frame. It can have as few as five couples who meet in their homes and pass around the responsibility of hosting and choosing a relevant couple issue and an exercise to go with it. Members can belong to the same congregation, live in the same zip code, or simply be acquaintances. New couples only come as visitors because this MEG is considered "closed" at least for one year.

The evening agreed-upon for the MEG to meet would begin with a sharing of Concerns and Celebrations, as good friends catch up with each other on events that have happened since their last meeting. This time is kept to a minimum so that the main couple exercise has adequate time for private discussion.

If any individual or couple is pre-occupied with a concern, the group lets the concern take priority. In one MEG, a father was concerned for his son traveling home from another state during a rainstorm. The group suggested he call his son to see if he had gotten home. He did and was able to report that the son had returned safely. The father felt great relief and ready to enjoy the MEG experience.

Often the host couple introduces the exercise for the evening. Couples then move to separate places in the home to discuss the exercise privately. After about half an hour (depending on the exercise) they come back together as a group and an important thing happens: public couple dialogue, like the Witnessing Dialogue, explained earlier by the Maces.

Here is where each couple discusses with the partner the impact of what they learned while doing the exercise or what they discovered about their relationship as they had their private dialogue. The couple speaks to each other but in the presence of the other couples as they all listen and learn the way that different couples address issues in their relationship. Sometimes the couple dialogue provokes a general discussion; sometimes not. No one gives advice, however. Experiences are the subject, not opinions or suggestions.

The group then calendars the next meeting date, and usually, there is simple refreshment provided by the host couple. The whole process takes no more than two hours.

Another kind of MEG is open to as many couples as choose to come and meets in a public place such as a business or a church. Couples usually sit around tables, if those are available, or arrange their chairs in circles. There is frequently a leader or facilitator couple for this kind of MEG, and that leader couple always does a public dialogue to help couples new to the group see the possibilities for their own later dialogues. Even though there may be many couples present, each couple is placed in a small group of no more than six couples.

The evening includes:

- couples meeting other couples at their table or circle,
- talking around the table or circle about a relevant but simple ice-breaker,
- a couple exercise done privately and knee-to-knee,
- a group time of interaction as couples process the exercise results in the whole group and share what they have learned.

Some couples have a public dialogue. Anniversaries often get celebrated with cupcakes or simple sweets, and there is usually some kind of snack available as well. As with the closed MEG, the time is kept to two hours.

Both kinds of MEGs adhere to some general guidelines:

- Each partner speaks only for self.
- All sharing is voluntary.
- All sharing is positive.

- Effective listening and talking skills are encouraged.
- No advice is given by any person to another.
- Confidentiality within the MEG builds trust.

Bobbye and Britton enthusiastically belong to both kinds of MEGs. They participate every month in a small closed MEG that meets in homes. This MEG was started when the Maces came to town decades ago and introduced the group concept for couples. Seventy-two couples were present on the evening that the Maces spoke, and seven MEGs were formed.

The Woods also leads several other MEGs which are open to any couple who chooses to come. Some of these MEGs meet in churches, some in non-profit counseling centers, some in businesses. All are responsible for much couple growth, as the following statements show (taken from couples' evaluations that followed an open MEG event).

Coming to the MEG has:

- transformed my marriage;
- provided priceless information;
- saved our friendship;
- made me more dependable;
- helped me talk about topics never discussed at home;
- led to my personal growth as a husband and father;
- brought fun back into our marriage;
- changed our empty-nester time to be regarded now as a grand, new adventure;
- made our conversation together interesting again; and
- made me value what I was about to give up on.

When one of the MEGs that the Woods lead was studied for a period of three years by a local state university graduate school, the results were startling about growth in identifiable skills. The couples who attended the MEG (and participated in the graduate department's research) found that they felt much more confident in handling conflicts, in the way they now talked to each other, and in general feelings of closeness and connection in their relationship.

The research also showed that of the 150+ couples who had responded to the monthly questions, there had been a divorce rate of only one percent. Granted it was a limited survey of couples and a time-span of only three years, but it does suggest the success of an intentional effort by couples to improve their relationship.

The Woods' Experience with Group Dialogue and MEGS

One September, Britton and Bobbye arrived at their closed MEG meeting to know that evening's subject for discussion was about Christmas. They were a bit puzzled since Christmas was still three months away, but they participated in the private couple exercise. There were questions such as "What usually happens that makes you feel like the Christmas season has really started?" and "What are some family traditions that you really like?" and even "What keeps you from enjoying Christmas celebrations?"

As the Woods discussed the questions, they had to agree that neither of them was satisfied with how they currently celebrated the season. Bobbye did all the decorating and the shopping, trimming the tree on the day after Thanksgiving. She did the holiday cooking and baking, and any entertaining related to the season. Britton waited until Christmas Eve and bought a few presents.

While they were doing the exercise, they discovered that they were both merely re-enacting the traditions and habits of the homes they grew up in. Bobbye's mother had done exactly what she was doing; Britton's family did not have a big celebration but bought a tree half-price on Christmas Eve, decorated it at that time, and gave only one present to each family member.

Their discovery about re-enacting the traditions of their families-of-origin seemed really important on that evening, and very quickly they made plans to change activities for the next Christmas to make sure they celebrated in a style that featured togetherness.

They made lists together; they intended to shop together; and the traditions they decided to share would be the ones they wanted. Identifying what had been happening made the next Christmas (and all those thereafter) much more enjoyable for both.

When the Woods joined the group after their private time, they learned that many of the couples had had some of the same experiences. Some of them, like the Woods, had spent the time deciding on the changes they would make to what had become a stressful holiday. One couple had even made a budget because they felt pressured by their family to spend more that was reasonable.

MEGs often offer such practical opportunities as this. As one husband told Britton, "we talk about things we never thought to deal with at home."

Couple Exercise

Sitting knee-to-knee (which means face-to-face and eye-to-eye), take turns talking about the following:

- Describe your first date.
- When did you know this relationship was something special?
- It is your wedding ceremony. Tell how you felt.
- Describe the first place you lived together.
- What was your favorite room and why?
- Choose one word that describes your first year together.

Recounting, remembering, and relieving common experiences is a good way to draw closer as a couple. The MEG is a place that often features this process as a way of sharing those events that have brought you to where you are today.

The Combined Bobbye and Britton Wood and David and Vera Mace Photo Album

1980s

Britton visits the Maces to set up the Mace Phonathon to all ACME Members

1980s

The Woods with the Maces when David and Vera came to Fort Worth to finalize research on their book, *Close Companions*. While in Fort Worth, they conducted one of their largest Retreats (72 couples).

1980s

The Maces with Bobbye in the Woods' Home.

1999

Kansas City, Bobbye and Britton are recipients of the David and Vera Mace Medal at the International Marriage Enrichment Conference (IMEC), Britton served as Conference Coordinator

1999

Mace Medal given in honor of David and Vera Mace, founders of ACME, this highest award is granted to a person or couple for distinguished service to marriage enrichment at a national or international level.

2016

Bobbye and Britton on their 60th anniversary

2016

The Woods' family at their 60th anniversary celebration

Strength 3

A Creative Use of Conflict

Two cups with the silhouettes of David and Vera were gifts during the Mace Phonathon to encourage Daily Couple Talk.

Chapter 11

The Philosophy of a Creative Use of Conflict

Couples often misunderstand that the way arguments are dealt with provides a clear indication of the quality of their relationship every day. One bitter fight unaddressed and unresolved can undo the pleasant effects of their special moments of intimacy and joy. That's why the Maces refer to using conflict creatively as the second "tool" in establishing and keeping growth goals on track.

It takes time to learn and to practice a new system for handling disagreements, but the payoffs are immediate. To resolve an argument without the usual lingering resentments and hard feelings gives both partners the sense that they have accomplished something worthwhile.

There is no way for two adults to live intimately and honestly in the same household and not have disagreements. That fact may be wearying and discouraging, especially if one or both partners insist on handling them with old, ineffective habits and techniques. But fortunately, most humans are complex, delightfully contradictory, and can decide and re-decide on just about every subject. Yes, there are some who seem to embrace a kind of resigned rigidity as they age, but most can change—if they have the right tools.

It is here at the time of anger and conflict that some couples say and do things that cripple their relationship for years, even if they stay together. When couples have run out of any ideas as to how to calmly address issues or disagreements, they often find that they have been practicing a portion of what the Maces called the "Love/Anger Cycle."

The Love Anger Cycle begins when couples are relating at a normal distance from each other and recognize that there is a difference between them regarding a specific issue. At this point, the couple notices that feelings have begun to well up within them (or in one of them). Their feelings are closer to the surface even though they have not been shared.

Both persons have now moved closer together with all their strong feelings present, but not yet expressed, a position that is right at the edge of resolution, but at this exact time if bad habits concerning conflict are used, the couple will not use the position to resolve the issue and move into intimacy.

Instead, both partners tend to escape all the way back to the safer level of difference. At the difference level they will cool off, and both may then feel so much better that they are reluctant to pursue the topic again. But the distance between them is once again wide and may continue to be so if they are reluctant to broach the subject of their difference again. Many couples at this point end up with an environment littered with subjects and issues that are unaddressed and unresolved.

They may even choose to accept a low-level of stress about the difference. It is here that some couples move into a safe and polite daily commerce that raises no threat of difference and disagreement. They choose to remain in the Love/Anger Cycle rather than explore the idea of creatively using conflict to grow the relationship.

Some couples try to tackle the topic again, but often with similar results. They not only do not get to intimacy, but they also feel that the Love/Anger Cycle has trapped them in a frustrating life pattern. What they need to do at *exactly this point* is the subject of many of the following chapters.

Anger is a healthy emotion that needs to be dealt with wisely. The Maces have designed a simple anger system to follow which breaks the unproductive cycle of the past (whatever the form it takes) and provides the way to diffuse the anger so the couple can deal with the issue. It offers them a new way:

- to share their feelings about the difference,
- to talk honestly to each other and listen empathetically,
- to gain a clearer understanding of the obstacle between them and why it is an obstacle,
- to negotiate a resolution of the disagreement, and
- to move into the sweet intimacy that all couples desire.

The resolution of the conflict and the closeness that comes from having learned and shared all the feelings related to the issue happens so quickly *that it readily becomes apparent why the Maces said, "Never waste a good conflict!"*

Love Anger Cycle

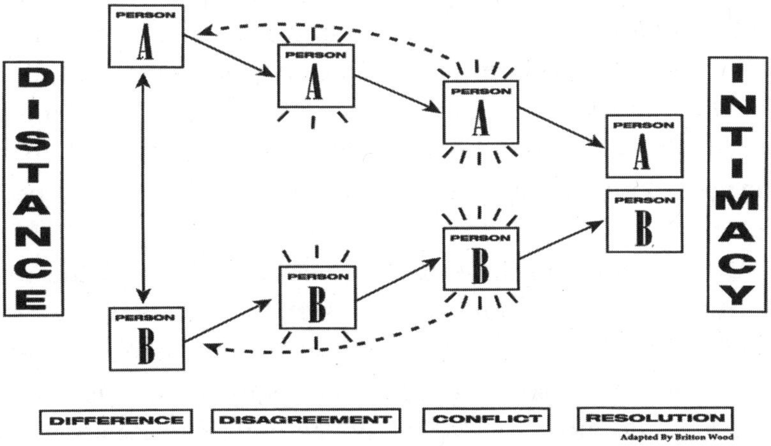

Using the Love/Anger Cycle is a way to reduce the negativity that often is the outcome of an argument that never gets resolved. It is a way to draw the couple together mentally and verbally. It is a way to diffuse anger. It is a fair and equitable way to begin the process of negotiation. It is team building. It gets rid of the need to be competitive, to "win" the argument no matter how. It provides a model for the future. It moves the couple to the important stage of collaboration.

The Woods' Experience with a Creative Use of Conflict

Often our styles of arguing, our attitudes toward disagreements, and the habits we have developed about engaging in them are brought into adulthood with us. We "caught" them in the homes where we were raised. We seldom ever think about those habits. Sometimes we are not even aware that we are using them.

But in few other areas does FOOIE show up so clearly as in the way we deal (or don't deal) with disagreements. Dr. Nancy Sanders was fond of using the term FOOIE, an acrostic for *Families of Origin Impact Everything.*

Bobbye grew up in a home where both parents agreed that the husband had the power. He made all decisions, handled the money (even though his wife taught school and had an income), and was the ultimate voice in settling all issues. In their arguments, Bobbye watched her mother apologize for everything that had led up to the disagreement, change the subject, offer food, and clearly remain unengaged. Both husband and wife had allowed this style to become habitual.

Without a conscious decision, Bobbye "caught" her mother's style. As a little girl, she did not say to herself, "This is how my mother handles conflict." She said, "This is how a woman handles conflict."

As she grew up, she noticed other styles of dealing with disagreements and analyzed them intellectually, but this is the style she always went to if she got angry or if someone was angry with her. This was her "training program" from her family-of-origin even though it often proved ineffective. When she and Britton married, this was the style that she tried to use in their arguments.

The problem was that Britton had had a different "training program" and thus had a different style of dealing with conflict. He had grown up watching his father slam down his newspaper and walk out, whenever there was a disagreement. Then his mother would sit down in a chair with a big and audible sigh, as though she were saying, "There is nothing we can do about this. Poor me. Look what I have to put up with."

Britton decided very early that this was not a profitable way to proceed. He decided that he would simply confront any conflict head-on; he would talk straight about whatever the issue was; and he would deal with it as quickly as possible. His reaction to the tableau in his family-of-origin was to set his own style and to use it when needed.

The Wood's two "training programs" did not match. And because there were many differences between them, as there are for every honest couple, there were occasional disagreements. Some of them even got heated up with anger and became a conflict. Then, Britton tried to confront and talk straight about the troubling issue; Bobbye tried to change the subject and avoid all anger by becoming very polite. Then they would each retreat back to a safe distance and wait for better feelings to replace those produced by the frustrations of never settling anything.

One "training program" was not automatically better or worse than another. One was possibly more productive, but an argument takes two people, and to resolve it there must be some measure of cooperation. These two "training programs" were simply what each had chosen, rarely thought about except at moments of disagreement.

The Maces' "tool" for handling conflict creatively came at just the right time for Bobbye and Britton. It gave them a method that both could use, a method just different enough from what they had each been practicing that both felt they were equally learning a new technique. Using it led to immediate changes that were so successful the Woods made an anger agreement to continue with this method. They each signed the agreement in as formal a manner as possible, to lend weight to its importance.

It is helpful to know there are options for changing old patterns of behavior. No one has to be locked into any pattern; we may be the products of the past (how could we not?), but we don't have to be prisoners. Becoming aware of what we are likely to do when we are angry is a good starting point for any desired changes in dealing with conflict. Without awareness, we do not have ANY options. We just act and react.

But even with awareness, there is also the need to change to something that fits for the individual couple. Each couple needs to discuss what training programs they both bring to their relationship, decide what can work for them, and discard the rest.

The Woods changed their style of handling arguments, especially Bobbye. However, that does not mean that the old style of avoidance and withdrawal are not there with her anymore. That old style is always a familiar option.

Awareness of its limitations gives Bobbye the freedom to consider another option. Choosing and using the Maces' style of regarding conflict as a friend to relationship provides a more flexible perspective for them with much more satisfaction.

Couple Exercise

Take turns responding to the following questions:

1. How did your mom (or the female who raised you) handle anger and conflict?
2. How did your dad (or the male who raised you) handle anger and conflict?
3. How do you handle anger and conflict today? Do you use one of these styles? Why or why not?
4. If you could make any change in handling conflict, what would it be?

Chapter 12
Handling Anger

Sometimes anger is the red-hot manifestation of high emotion, with loud voices, harsh words, and violent actions. At other times anger is the white-hot avoidance that stuffs all acknowledgment inside and suffers in gut-wrenching silence while it warns everyone away with hostile looks.

Whether anger is turned on others or on oneself, the way it is unsuccessfully handled over time can cause divisions, attacks, hard feelings, hostility, casualties, and loss of health. And it often happens in families.

The Dear Abby column is often full of poignant letters seeking advice or support about family estrangements and divisions. "I haven't spoken to my sister in thirty years," a letter might begin. "I always return my mother's letters and gifts unopened ever since we argued about _____," another might report. Stressful events such as deaths and probating wills have caused such anger and conflict in some families that they never recover their former friendships.

Sometimes it is stranger anger that involves others. We live in such a dangerous world that someone else's anger or animosity can cause harm, as in the horrible massacres at schools, churches and synagogues, nightclubs, or concerts. At the very least, stranger anger can delay flights or seal off shopping centers.

Coming home from the airport one day after picking up their grandson Will for a visit, Britton and Bobbye's car was forced to a standstill, as were all the cars going both east and west on the Interstate, because a young man was standing close to the railing of a bridge crossing the highway, threatening to jump. The young man had been there for such a long time that he caused a traffic jam that lasted for hours, inconvenienced travelers, and delayed appointments.

The young man was distraught because of a fight with his girlfriend. With no ideas about how to settle this frustrating situation, he ran out on the bridge and threatened suicide. Finally, a SWAT team arrived, reasoned with him, rescued him from danger, and allowed the miles of frustrated and anxious drivers to move on.

It is a sad example of why society needs some ideas about how to deal with anger, especially in families, where destructive and unfair behavior can get carried into the next generations because of the family's importance to healthy growth and development.

Here is what the Maces said about an Anger Agreement (or Contract) for couples and why they felt it was a key ingredient or "tool" in a long-term, healthy relationship:

> ***David:*** In a close relationship there are two simple words: love and anger. One word moves you toward intimacy and one word moves you away. One feeling draws you toward each other, and the other pulls you apart. All other words are just variations of those words—love and anger.
>
> You have no foundation on which to proceed in an intimate relationship until you have a solemn contract or policy concerning how to handle angry interactions. Without a contract, agreement, or policy, it is easy to just slip back into old ways of doing things, the very ways that got the couple into messes before.

There is no way a person can deal with these situations without walking right up to them with a policy that both have agreed on previously. One of the basic conditions of intimacy is a long-term contract regarding anger. Without it, one or the other can just walk away or continue to use methods and systems of anger that do not work in this relationship.

You've got to have tools with which to work. If your car breaks down on the road, you've got to have tools and you have to know how to use the tools. Or you have to get to a garage and find someone who knows how to use the tools. That's why we have remedial services. But nine-tenths of the time couples can work through the situation themselves if they have a contract or policy and know how to use the tools. My goal is to give every couple a set of tools. *Those tools for dealing with anger are the key to it all.*

Britton: So, the couple has a contract for dealing with anger. Are there some specifics in that contract?

David: Yes. The first specific is that *we give each other full permission to be angry with each other.* We might as well, because every couple is going to be angry sometime. Anger is a healthy emotion. It is not something disgraceful, something to be ashamed of. We do not create it. Anger always comes as a response to a stimulus, real or imagined. The important thing is to acknowledge it to yourself and know that it can be a useful and instructive thing.

Every human gets angry. If they don't, there is something gravely abnormal about them. Anger is good. It is a person's survival kit, a lifesaver. I once met a man who said to me, "You are a Quaker. You know about eliminating anger through the discipline of meditation." And I said to him, "I don't want to eliminate anger. My anger is a dynamic part of me, and I don't want to lose it. *I want to use it for growth.*"

The second specific of the anger contract is that *when either of us is angry with the other, we will say so.* I spent many futile experiences in the early days of our marriage trying to deal with anger in the only ways I knew: venting it or suppressing it. Unreasonably I felt that when I was angry with Vera, I needed to get away from her. I was afraid of what my anger might do to her. I would go off by myself and try to deal it with alone. But with all the stuff boiling inside of me, it took me hours to get myself into a better frame of mind. Then when I felt better, I came back.

But the issue was never dealt with, you see. I didn't even tell Vera about it; I just made excuses for going away. But this way of dealing with it was actually driving me further away from Vera. I couldn't get her understanding. I couldn't get her love. I thought I had to do it all myself. It was a way around a problem that besets everyone, but it was not a healthy way.

Running away from our anger does not nurture the healing process that can take place in a relationship when you can spill out your feelings and both can hear them. *Sharing your feelings is what begins the process of understanding each other.* At that time, I thought it would be a weakness to talk to Vera about my anger. I didn't want her to see me in that kind of role. I wanted to be strong and self-sufficient, dealing with my anger capably.

Now I don't run away. I don't cut myself off from the healing resources of relationship. Now when I get angry, I just come to Vera and tell her. Together we talk about it, and I get the healing and support I need.

I have learned that we need to communicate anger as soon as possible before it gets worse. If it is too hot to handle at that moment or if there are other people present and the timing is not right for discussion, we will set an appointment. *The processing of the anger will be more productive when both of us can discuss the issue rationally.*

And a side benefit is that when you handle it this way, you can merely acknowledge the anger and state what is going on inside you. When you do it in this order, it instills a kind of confidence that anger WILL be dealt with. Knowing that you are going to address the subject that resulted in the anger allows you to avoid building up the heat. When you know this, you don't have to get angrier.

Vera: The contract is that you will make an appointment to deal with it as soon as possible. You treat it as a serious situation and say something like, "Can we deal with this issue tonight at 7:00, 10:00, or a convenient time?" This way both of you know that you are going to talk about it and not just put it on a shelf and ignore it.

David: The important thing is that you let no anger build up between each other. Setting an appointment allows both to know that you are going to deal with the situation. Without addressing it, it simply allows the anger to become attached to the next disagreement and makes dealing with it even more complicated.

If you don't clear up the anger situations as they come, they will accumulate; you will find yourself saying unreasonable things like "I know for a fact you did (or said) this another time, and it means you are going to be just like your mother."

Britton: It is also possible that without clearing it up with the person involved, you may simply unload the anger onto some unsuspecting person and thus create even more complications. This happens often in businesses, I think, where one person takes out on his associates the anger that he feels toward some family member.

Bobbye: This contract thing about setting an appointment is interesting, because if I know that at our appointment we are going to deal with the angry situation, and I will get a chance at that time to convey what I think and feel, I can see that its purpose can be freeing. I can take down defenses because we have a kind of treaty. I know that it is going to be a process that will include me and my feelings, and that reassures me that it has a chance for a hearing.

David: Yes. It's like having a raincoat with you as you are walking in the mountains. You don't have to worry when the dark clouds come because you know you can use the raincoat if you need it. Once the contract has been established, and once you begin to put it into practice, then you have reached the stage that you are secure against the damage that anger can do. In fact, you are using the anger situation to actually improve your relationship.

Many times, in the groups we lead, Vera and I are asked to discuss how we handled our last anger situation. And it's hard to find one because once you use the contract to clear up the situation and the anger it caused, the angry scenes become fewer and fewer. When you are free from the threat that anger can have, you are free to be intimate.

The important thing is to deal with every conflict as it arises, or as soon as possible. A continuing state of anger becomes resentment, a low-key continuing state of hostility. It is my observation over many years of marriage counseling that people who suppress or try to ignore their anger eventually destroy their ability to be tender. Suppressing the anger and subscribing to the idea of "peace at any price" will eventually undermine all the good feelings of the relationship.

Bobbye: The first parts of the contract are that you give each other permission to be angry and you express that anger both to yourself and to your partner. Then you move into a discussion of the situation, or if that is not appropriate at the time, you set an appointment for the discussion. What would be the next step?

David: The third specific of the contract is that *when we are angry, we will not attack each other.* A person is much more likely to enter into a conversation about the angry situation if he or she is not going to be attacked and knows it. There is no need for that person to be defensive, no need to brace for what may follow, since each person has agreed to this part of the contract. It is reassuring and builds confidence in the process.

Instead of an attack (and usually a counter-attack) *neither partner holds the other responsible for the anger of the other but agrees that the anger now belongs to the relationship.* Anger can blind you to where the other person is. Addressing the situation without an attack allows you a better chance to find out what was really going on.

Both must work it out together. One cannot go off and clear it up alone; it is a joint task. Clearing up anger is the task of the relationship. Get behind the anger and you are more likely to find out what is really going on. And another benefit is that clearing up the anger gives an opportunity to understand each other better. That is no small benefit.

Britton: I understand that you need to acknowledge the anger to each other (even if it just belongs to one partner), that both must agree not to attack each other, and that clearing up anger is the joint responsibility of the relationship. Is there something else?

David: Yes. Up to this point, the steps in the contract have been mostly what we will and will not do, what we will and will not say. The next step in the process actually involves communication and how to use it most effectively.

It is important to use communication to deal with the feelings each of us has. Without sharing the feelings, you just discuss information that both of you know, information that may have led to the conflict in the first place. *By sharing the feelings, you begin to get to the heart of the issue.* Only then can you begin negotiation and come to a workable compromise. And you are dealing with the issue at the level of a disagreement, without the anger and without the high emotions of a conflict.

Bobbye: I remember the first Marriage Enrichment Retreat we went to. I was struck by this very point of sharing feelings. It had not been a part of our communication in the past, and I was intrigued by the possibility for us. I said so in the evaluation at the end of the retreat and, as I remember, I wrote rather glowing evaluations about freeing each other up to share feelings.

Then when we were driving home, Britton said to me, "I'm feeling apprehensive about going back to work tomorrow after being away." And I said, "You shouldn't feel that way." Then we discussed what he could say should anyone at work even mention being gone over a Sunday. It was long after we got home, visited with our daughters, and re-entered our typical schedules that I replayed in my mind Britton's statement, "I am feeling apprehensive." Hours had passed and neither of us had taken any opportunity to discuss those feelings. It was so much out of our normal patterns of conversation that neither of us even noticed.

Britton: Yes, we went right to problem-solving, which was our normal route to take in conversation. Sharing feelings was difficult for us when it was out of the familiar route our discussions tended to take.

David: Yes, the sharing of feelings is a long step for couples to take who have never done it together and who are not accustomed to it. Feelings are your spontaneous response to your awareness of what is going on within you and around you. You do not manufacture your feelings. They are your authentic reaction to your life and what is going on in your world.

Bobbye: Can't you manufacture your feelings? Suppose you want to feel self-pity or a sense of inadequacy? Can't you just create a situation or circumstance that will produce the feeling that you wish to have?

David: Yes, but you are just manufacturing the situation, not the feelings. Feelings cannot be manufactured. You are only creating a stimulus to which the feelings you want is a response. But the feelings themselves are authentic. They are your real response from the inner "you" to the outside world.

But we know that sharing feelings is difficult for many couples. That is why in our retreats we often ask couples to share with each other as many feelings as they can. We usually ask this as we are introducing the subject of handling disagreements or conflicts in a new way. It becomes a warmup for those couples who have had little practice in using this form of communication, especially as a tool for resolving disagreements or conflicts.

Britton: We also have recently had a good illustration of the use of sharing feelings to help resolve the conflict. It was over the subject of magazines.

Bobbye: Oh, yes. And it happened on the day after the retreat that I mentioned earlier. As long as we have been married, we have had a difference over magazines. Britton likes them and tends to subscribe to many. I do not.

So, on the day after we returned home from the retreat, I cleaned house, which also meant throwing away all the out-of-date issues that were lying around. When Britton came home from work that evening, all the old magazines were gone into outside trash cans, except for two that were in a wastebasket in the den. Unfortunately, they were professional journals which Britton had not had time to read yet.

Britton: And I asked, "Why did you throw away my magazines?"

Bobbye: You said it in a loud voice, which was unlike you. And I did not like the question. So, I asked in an equally loud voice, "What makes you think they are YOUR magazines?" Clearly, our difference overtaking and keeping magazines was moving to the level of a disagreement.

Britton: So, I answered in a way to shut down the disagreement: "Because I paid for them!"

Bobbye: That was SO unfair. I taught school, earned a salary, and considered myself a financial partner. I realized that our disagreement was moving toward a conflict, a position that I usually just ignored, then went away and stewed about.

But this time I realized that I had an option in how to continue, in fact, several of them. It felt familiar to just check out of the argument, my usual strategy. I could tell him, "OK, those magazines can stack up to the ceiling as far as I care. I won't touch another one." But that was a lie.

Another option was that I could cry because he yelled at me and I didn't deserve it. But I told myself that was weak, and I would not be able to cry and argue at the same time. Or I could try a different technique than I had ever used before. That was one I had learned at the retreat. That was to share our feelings about the subject.

Well, right then was not the time to do it, since by that time we were both really angry, so we let some time go by. I guess you would refer to that as setting an appointment for later. Then I went into the den where Britton was sitting and asked him if he would like to talk about his feelings about magazines. And he said he would.

Britton: Yes, but that wasn't all there was to it. A contributing factor was that you asked very tenderly if I wanted to talk about our feelings about magazines. If you had asked me harshly or sarcastically, I probably would not have agreed to do it. It was out of our normal pattern. But you asked softly, and I too had been intrigued with this technique at the retreat. I swallowed my pride and said yes.

Also, at the retreat, we had made a very solemn commitment to growth. Part of my saying yes was acknowledging that commitment, even though at the time I had little idea of what that meant.

Bobbye: So, we went into the bedroom, shut the door, and got ready for a conversation about our feelings about magazines. Neither of us knew what to say. What could you feel about a magazine? But we stuck with it and were both shocked with where it came out.

I discovered that I felt fearful that the magazines were a symbol that Britton was going to be like his father. On the

Thanksgiving, before we married, I had gone to visit Britton's parents and had taken a mental snapshot of what I considered to be a very junky house, full of newspapers and magazines and many forms of broken appliances.

I was learning that Britton's father was a packrat who did not like to get rid of anything. You could not even get a glass out of the kitchen cabinet for a drink of water because of all the stacks of unusable utensils. I later learned to love Britton's father and to respect him. But at that time, I was shocked. I was determined that my house would never look like that. I was afraid that people would think I was a terrible housekeeper.

Britton: Yes, but you never know when you are going to need some of those things. However, I agree that my parents' home was very messy.

Bobbye: The snapshot I took alarmed me and made me ruthless about throwing things away, including magazines, which I considered junky and unneeded. I felt righteous as an efficient housekeeper who did a good job. I did not want anyone to criticize my work, as I defined it.

Britton: And after a while of considering her feelings, I remembered an episode from childhood when we moved from Shreveport, Louisiana, to Beaumont, Texas. I had a big barrel of toys and they did not get moved with us. I was not asked to pick out two or three toys. I did not get a choice at all.

I grew up feeling that I should have a choice in the things that I believed belonged to me. I still feel that way. I am upset and alarmed when I do not get a choice.

Bobbye: We were both astonished. We had entered the bedroom willing to try a new strategy but uncertain about how to proceed. There was not a lot of trust or confidence. But the exchange of feelings had changed the mood.

Now there was tenderness and a willingness to compromise, to work on the issue that had initially caused the argument. I could certainly understand how a little boy would feel without his toys. Britton understood my need for a clean house with no stacks of old magazines.

The differences between us were still there and probably always will be, even after many conversations. But at that point, there was a different attitude and much more of a desire to cooperate.

In thirty seconds, we worked out a plan for what we would do in the future. I had permission to throw away the magazines that came weekly. Britton would tear out the articles that he wanted to save but not keep the whole journal. And the magazines that I didn't know what to do with, I would stack by his side of the bed. That way he could not even get in bed without acknowledging that these were on their way out if he did not exercise choice. The solution lasted for years until recycling came along.

But the real progress was in our growing recognition that sharing feelings was a productive way to handle conflicts.

David: That is a beautiful, classical illustration which we will quite likely use without acknowledgment.

Bobbye: Go right ahead, because it is the principle you are teaching here that is so important and productive. The magazines are just a typical area of disagreement. What we learned from exercising a new technique about handling disagreements or conflicts by sharing what we felt about them is what needs to be emphasized. What we learned was so different from what we had been practicing before that it caught us both by surprise.

Vera: You both developed a coping tool through communication, this time through the sharing of feelings about a difference. Thus, you were able to move toward an understanding and through that door you moved toward intimacy. I too used this tool when I discovered a very annoying difference between David and me.

For example, I am a "day" person. I like to get up early, and that's the time of day that I have the most energy. David is a "night" person. He likes to stay up late and sleep late in the morning. It is simply a difference in rhythms, but one that I did not know about when we married.

David: A disagreement is often about differences. But until the difference moves to the level of a disagreement, there is really no need to address it. When Vera got annoyed enough to speak up and insist that I get out of bed at an earlier hour, the issue had moved to the level of a disagreement.

We then began to pay attention and to use the anger contract. She thought that my staying in bed was disrupting the whole household. I thought that I had worked late in the night and needed my sleep.

Vera: So, we shared our feelings about the situation and after that, we moved quickly to negotiation. As I remember, the compromise was that David said he would not sleep late every day, and I said that I would accept that when he did sleep late, it was because he needed extra sleep. It satisfied both of us.

Britton: Is negotiation part of the anger contract?

David: Negotiation is the step you use when you have satisfactorily dealt with the feelings of each partner. Negotiation is where you try to come to terms with the disagreement and where you discuss what each partner might do (or might not do) that would be helpful. However, there is no use jumping to negotiation until both partners feel heard and understood. If you move too soon to possible solutions, they will more than likely not be fulfilled.

You cannot negotiate a conflict. You can only negotiate the disagreement behind the conflict. *A conflict is a disagreement heated up with anger, and when you are heated up, you are not in a negotiating mood.* Take the heat out and you can deal with it more logically.

Britton: That sounds both simple and complex at the same time. Yet so many people see conflict as negative, something to stay away from. Do you see moving the definition of conflict into a more positive light as the same thing as behavior modification?

David: Basically, it is a change of attitude and that in itself opens the door to behavior modification. Feelings, for example, are often based on attitudes. If you can change the attitudes, then the same stimuli will produce different feelings

Vera: What is the difference between attitudes and feelings?

David: The attitude is what triggers off the mindset that produces the feelings. If you think the world is a hostile place, you will feel that everybody is out to get you. But if you think the world is a friendly place, you will feel that it is safe to reveal yourself and to interact with others.

The attitude is not the feeling. It is an evaluation. And when you change your attitude, you also change the feelings that are produced from your evaluation. The attitude is the mindset, the way you evaluate what you see.

You cannot change your attitude just by examining your feelings. That is a different process. You see, you don't produce your feelings. They are your inner responses to what you believe—your mindset—about what you are experiencing. They are the expression of what your experience signifies for you. If you can change what your experience signifies for you, the feelings will themselves change.

If we can change our attitudes toward the word conflict, we are better able to go through the process to get to the place of negotiation. There are at least three attitudes toward anger:

1. The first one is, "This is bad; run away from it."
2. The second one is, "This is unavoidable, and you must simply endure it. It is a part of life."
3. And the third one is, "This is a growth point; use it!"

This is the attitude that locates conflict as a possibility for the growth of the relationship and is the only really productive way to handle it.

The Woods' Experience with Handling Anger

Many couples bring with them into marriage old ways and methods of handling angry scenes that come to all couples. Harville Hendrix and Helen Hunt refer to those ways and methods as being on "autopilot." The couples simply act without thinking of options or consequences, but when they do, they are robbing themselves of a way to maintain the things that all couples want and need: loving support, safety, understanding, and intimacy.

"Autopilot" requires no thought. It requires no analysis of what is really happening and no understanding of what each person wants to happen. Like most couples, "Autopilot" is what Britton and Bobbye brought into their marriage from the "training programs" they observed in their families of origin.

About twenty years into the marriage, the Woods, modeling largely on what they had learned from the Maces' Anger Contract, wrote out an agreement about how they would handle anger. Each of them signed it, as though it were a legal document. Each knew that it was important and would bring a new level of understanding into their relationship. Here is the contract they signed so solemnly and hopefully:

1. ACKNOWLEDGE YOUR ANGER TO YOURSELF and give yourself and your partner permission to have that anger. Ignoring, evading, or denying your own feelings only postpones beginning the process and often causes us to involve others.

Most people can merely bypass this step, knowing exactly what they feel, but for people like Bobbye—who had chosen a circuitous route for avoiding conflict—this step is necessary.

2. TELL YOUR PARTNER ABOUT YOUR ANGER. If an adult "time-out" (insightfully labeled by Dr. Scott Stanley) is needed in order to calm down, say so. Use "I" statements and assign no blame. "You are making me mad" is not the same as "I am angry."

   If the time for dealing with the anger is not appropriate at the moment, set an appointment. Keep that appointment as eagerly as you would keep a dentist's appointment to deal with a severe toothache.
3. NEITHER PARTNER HOLDS THE OTHER RESPONSIBLE FOR THE ANGER EACH ONE FEELS BUT AGREES THAT THE ANGER NOW BELONGS TO THE RELATIONSHIP. It is the joint task of the relationship to deal with the disputed issue and to clear up the anger by talking about it together.
4. AVOID ATTACKS. They only lead to counter-attacks, defense, and more hard feelings. They make it unlikely that this disputed issue will really be settled to the satisfaction of either partner.
5. SHARE FEELINGS about the subject and REALLY LISTEN to each other. Feelings are often a part of the issue and need to be heard. They do not have to be logical or in a symmetrical order. But they do need attention.

   Each partner chooses to paraphrase what they hear so that the partner *knows* what was heard. Do not edit and do not debate. Do not try to explain. Putting your partner's words into your own words does not mean you agree with them, only that you have heard them.
6. When both partners have shared the feelings and indicate that there is understanding, then MOVE TO NEGOTIATION for settlement of the issue. Not until there is a real understanding of each other's position will this be possible, but when the conflict has moved back to the level of a mere disagreement, there is a chance to explore options through negotiation.

Couple Exercise

You do have a choice in how you deal with anger

As a couple, you can look at the Woods' Anger Agreement and change what is important to your relationship.

Bobbye and Britton's Anger Agreement

1. Acknowledge your anger to yourself.
2. Tell your partner that you are angry.
3. Assume that one person cannot be totally responsible for the anger you feel.
4. Agree to be non-harmful to each other in a verbal, physical, or emotional way.
5. Agree to a time to listen to the feelings of the angry person that is fair to both of you.
6. Allow the angry person to share all feelings possible without interruption.
7. After both persons have shared what each feels and let the other know what feelings have been heard, then both agree to a time for negotiation to take place.

Now consider these questions:

1. What changes would you make in styling your own anger agreement?
2. What is an issue in your relationship that could benefit from some discussion?

> ***"The health of any . . . the couple, can be seen as a function of its ability to negotiate conflicts." From Conflict to Resolution***
>
> ***—Susan M. Heitler, PhD.***

Your signatures:

Chapter 13
The Effect of Anger-as-Power

Little babies alone in their cribs often scream in rage, understandable for ones so absolutely dependent on others to meet basic needs. What is not so understandable in the ones so young is the listening pause between the screams. It seems to be a pause that measures whether those screams are going to be effective in bringing a response from the baby's weary caretakers. Could this be a power struggle in the very first weeks of life?

Young children early learn how to use tumultuous and very noisy public scenes to get what they want. Many of us have witnessed screaming, kicking tantrums at the grocery store when an angry toddler is confronted with mommy's "no" about candy tantalizingly stacked on shelves. The tantrum is an early test of where the power is going to lie, and the fact that the tantrum is done in public may be calculated. Could it be a dress rehearsal of the Anger-as-Power Show before it goes on tour and plays in many venues as life moves on?

Adolescents often use whining, pouting, unfair bargaining, constant challenges, moody rebellions, shouting, and annoying questions of "Why?" in hopes of forcing harassed parents into compliance.

It is no wonder that many people who have used one or more of these examples of Anger-as-Power often come to adulthood with a firm belief that displays of anger are an easy and efficient way to bend others to their will. The goal is to win; the goal is to get others to acquiesce. The goal is to get what they want—and all of what they want. The goal is to win any argument, challenge, or disagreement with whatever form of Anger-as-Power that has been successful in the past.

When people get married who have successfully used the idea of Anger-as-Power, there is often the hidden expectation that bending someone to their will can still be used as a tool to achieve a personal agenda. That agenda and how to get it accomplished may be more artfully disguised than babies, children, and adolescents can manage. However, the knowledge of how to use that tool successfully is always right under the surface and can come out in times of stress or perceived threat to the desired outcome.

The adult idea of shared power and the equality of agendas is regarded as an unrealistic ideal, rarely considered in the heat of a conflict. The old and well-tried idea of Anger-as-Power is far too familiar not to use. When Anger-as-Power needs to control not only the situation, but the relationship, it becomes abusive and can become destructive to both person and the relationship.

However, if couple enjoyment and couple closeness are goals worth reaching, changes in handling conflicts need to be considered and practiced. New chosen boundaries need to be agreed upon and practiced by the couple.

The Maces were well-acquainted in dealing with the issue of Anger-as-Power. They considered it a crucial habit to be overcome and developed their own anger method as a central "tool" for replacement. Here is what they had to say about anger and power:

> ***David:*** You have to ask yourself continually if you are using anger to clear up a confrontational situation, or if you are using it to gain personal power. Some people see anger as a powerful

weapon which they have to fight for their rights. Vera and I say that it is not a useful weapon.

First, it makes the other person hold on stubbornly to their point of view, and second, it will never get you to a close connection with another person. In fact, Anger-as-Power demonstrations almost always lead to alienation and distance. So, you have to ask yourself why you are holding onto your anger and using it as a kind of weapon against others. You must ask yourself if you are really accomplishing what you most want.

If all you want to do is win an argument, then you can certainly accomplish that, but if you want to establish and grow a relationship with someone you love, demonstrations of Anger-as-Power will not work. You must develop another style of dealing with anger.

Britton: I have known administrators and business managers who use anger to control their subordinates and employees. They use anger to keep things running smoothly—as THEY would define smoothly.

David: Yes, this often happens in companies. However, I do not think it is appropriate in intimate relationships because the cost is too high. *What you pay is not worth what you get. You may get your way, you may even feel proud of the power you demonstrate, but at a high price.*

If I get angry with Vera and express my anger forcefully, something will probably get done. But the angry fight will leave feelings of resentment, and these may go on for a very long time.

But if I get angry with Vera and tell her about it, and we proceed through the steps of the anger contract, things will also get done—and without the pain and the wounds. It's a question of taking a hard look at yourself and the kind of relationship you want to achieve in marriage.

Bobbye: Are you saying that Anger-as-Power is counter-productive in intimate relationships?

David: Definitely. And I am saying further that steering the anger into a technique that addresses the fears and frustrations that underlie the anger is a much more sensible approach. But it is not a technique that is built into our human nature; it is a point at which we rise above our nature—and our habits. And we must make that choice to rise above.

We must recognize what are our primitive impulses and handle them better. It's like learning good table manners instead of grabbing our food with our fingers. We still eat, but we have learned a technique that makes eating more gracious, which involves others in wanting to have a conversation while we eat together.

Similarly, we can begin to see the destructive outcomes of anger and begin to find more sensible ways to redirect it. Neither temper tantrums nor fierce denial of anger will gain the growth that produces heartfelt satisfaction in a relationship.

Britton: You are referring to a creative use of anger and conflict, a channeling of anger to produce a situation that can benefit both people involved? Are you also saying that avoiding Anger-as-Power is more likely to lead to couple growth?

David: Learning to handle and redirect anger is one way to growth. Growth can come in many ways, many of them quite pleasant. However, the kind of growth that handling anger makes possible is pretty basic. *Conflict and anger pinpoint the areas where our growth is blocked.*

If we ignore or avoid those areas, growth may go on elsewhere, but it will be hampered and hindered in the openness and closeness and cooperation that we have with each other. Conflict and anger merely show the areas where work needs to be done.

Britton: Do you have an example of how the two of you have misused anger and then redirected it to a more positive outcome?

Vera: Perhaps this might be an illustration. Would the situation in South Africa about the big box of dried milk be a good example? What do you think, David?

David: I think that would be good.

Vera: Well, let me give some details about it. Before David had his heart attack, the carrying of luggage had never been a difficulty. But everything changed after the heart attack. He was not supposed to lift or carry heavy things, and I have never been good at it. I don't like to carry heavy things, and David has always done that.

We also had to make certain dietary adjustments, such as taking certain food that David was going to need when we went on trips to other countries. Because we were going to be in South Africa for an extended period, we took powdered milk with us, not knowing if milk would be readily available where we would be staying.

It was toward the end of our stay, and I insisted that we go to a grocery store to pick up a few supplies. I saw a big package of powdered milk and knew we needed it. It was rather large and different from the ones we had originally brought, so I stopped to read the contents on the box. And David got very angry with me.

David: Yes, I was angry, and I used my anger as power. First, I took the grocery cart and walked away with it. Then I even walked out of the store, expecting that she would follow me, which she did. I told myself that I was doing this because Vera likes to spend time in stores. When she does, she buys things and our luggage just grows and grows until it becomes unmanageable. Neither of us would be able to carry it. Also, she was dawdling, a habit I do not like. She was also wasting time by reading some big box labels about contents that I thought we did not need anyway.

Vera: I don't really dawdle. I just move at my own pace.

David: But the point is that I angrily walked out of the grocery store and returned to the hotel, which was quite nearby. It was clear that this was a hot situation that we needed to clear up.

Vera: As soon as we got back into our room at the hotel, David began to explain what was going on inside of him, and I did the same—a procedure that had worked well for us in the past.

I told him I felt manipulated because he took the grocery cart away, knowing that I could not carry that big box of powdered milk. I felt hurt that he had walked out of the store, ignoring the fact that we needed milk and that the milk was for HIM. I also felt hurt that he had assumed that I was not doing all the reading of contents from the best of motives. And I felt hurt that he had left the store and just expected me to follow.

David: And I explained what was going on inside of me. I felt embarrassed that I was forced to let Vera lift heavy things and carry heavy luggage. I used to be called the family donkey because even though I was small, I was wide and strong and could carry enormous weights. Now after the heart attack, that ability was all gone, and I missed it. I could have dealt with the fact that Vera was once again dawdling, but because I felt that she was doing so in order to increase the weight of our luggage—that was just over the top.

Britton: This seems like an illustration that a conflict is sometimes made up of more than one thing.

Bobbye: Yes, a checkbook that doesn't balance can be a disputed part of an issue, one fairly easy to resolve when both partners are engaged. But often, around that simple factor are other factors and attitudes, such as, "You spend too much money and you always have."

This sounds like there was the issue of different rhythms; there was the issue of walking away from the grocery store and leaving one person behind, and there was the issue of the purchase of the milk.

Vera: Yes, but the most important thing was that I felt I had been misunderstood. I had thought that I had been doing all of this to please David, to help take care of him. Then he treated it as though I was undermining his health. I knew that we needed the milk. I had checked before we ever left the hotel room.

David: All of this came out as we shared our feelings with each other. *Without the discussion of each one's point of view and the feelings involved, we would have left out necessary information that helped each of us understand the other.* If we had not "worked it through" by sharing our feelings about all parts of the issue, we would have been left with only my Anger-as-Power actions of walking away with the grocery cart.

This alone caused hard feelings between us and would have continued to. But because we had a way to process what each of us was feeling, we understood each other. That was more important than anything else about this circumstance.

I also learned that I was wrong about the need for milk. I got up early the next morning, went to the grocery store, and bought the very box of dried milk that we had been arguing over. It was one way of apologizing for a misunderstanding about the milk.

Britton: I think your dried milk situation was a great illustration of how you took a complicated event and turned it into an example of how getting to the feelings and really listening to them can make both partners more aware of each other.

We are hearing a story of how you put into practice a philosophy that can sound academic at times. Yet it is a rather typical situation for most couples, and *it is very encouraging to see how an angry scene can be handled to lead to growth.*

Vera: And this is the real nature of growth, awareness of ourselves and of each other.

Britton: Can the use of Anger-as-Power over time affect the intimacy and tenderness a couple feels for each other?

David: Does the unchecked and calculated use of Anger-as-Power have an effect on the everyday intimacy exchanges between a couple? Absolutely. Does dealing with the anger issues in a systematic way automatically produce tenderness? The answer is no. What it does is clear away the rabid weed that is anger, which destroys the places where tenderness grows. It's almost as if you were growing an exotic flower in your garden, and you were not sure it was going to come up. You've got to keep the weeds away from it because they could overwhelm it and steal the nutrients in the soil.

You must deal with the angry situations as they come up—and you must not use anger as a weapon or a badge of power. In order to clear out a place for the flower to bloom with its sweet tenderness, you have to find mutually helpful ways to deal with anger. *When you reduce the number of toxic situations by clearing them up, you are giving tenderness a chance.*

Vera: Are you saying that we were not tender before we chose a new way of handling anger?

David: Yes, we were. At least you were. You had the willingness and the ability. But it wasn't until I got my anger dealt with that I could really be free to be tender with you.

In practice, at least in terms of the impact, the emotions of love and the emotion of hostility cannot coexist over time. Hostility and anger will trample all efforts to harbor tender, gentle, and intimate feelings.

You cannot be angry and loving at the same time. The presence of Anger-as-Power is damaging to love. Even the threat of anger is harmful to love. But when anger is cleared up by using a system that works, it dissipates. It takes the threat away and allows you to use the issue purposefully. And it allows tenderness and intimacy to grow. *Tenderness is a by-product of the removal of anger.*

The Maces repeatedly used an illustration of the difference between agencies of Intervention and agencies of Prevention. They wanted to show which side their work stood on when it came to the results of anger. It was a fine line they often walked, as they worked on the side of Prevention and Enrichment but knew experientially the side of intervention.

Intervention agencies, they said, are like the ambulance and police that have to be called when a car did not successfully negotiate a sharp curve on a mountain road, and there was a terrible wreck. Intervention agencies include Law Enforcement, Child Protective Services, courts, attorneys, domestic violence facilities, and anger management counseling.

Prevention agencies are the signs along the mountain road that picture the curve ahead and notify drivers about its dangers. Prevention agencies are trying to prevent damage and injury by becoming the dispensers of helpful information to schools, churches, businesses, and families. They are counselors, therapists, educators, and mediators—those who regularly deal with couples who can use that information to form better and more productive unions than they have been experiencing.

The Woods' Experience with a Resolution of Anger

Many conflicts settled with the Anger Agreement can undermine the power of old habits, even when those habits occasionally intrude on the present. Many couples, including the Woods, have overcome habits and attitudes to arrive at a workable agreement that produces much better effects than what they originally tried to practice. The way couples deal with anger is very much a habit, like putting on the left shoe first every morning or insisting on only a particular brand of toothpaste. Old habits can be overcome with awareness, attention, and a desire to replace them with something that shows to be more effective.

Britton came home from tennis one Saturday morning recently, tired from the hottest temperatures of the early summer, as well as from a strenuous game of doubles. Bobbye felt the heat as well, having worked all morning weeding and pruning in the flower garden.

She was sitting on the ground filling up the final yard sack with dead leaves and letting the hose run on newly composted plants. The heat was just about to be too much for continuing when Britton stepped out of the house onto a brick walkway around the garden. He saw pools of water on the ground and yelled at her, "Where did all this water come from?"

Bobbye heard that question as criticism, since this was a habit they had struggled with before, when Britton was prone to point out the imperfections in her gardening. She was getting too hot, he would say, or she had not put the tools up properly, or she had not trimmed in a thorough manner. As the one doing the gardening work, Bobbye would object.

Though the criticism had not happened in a long time, Bobbye still remembered its effects and thought she was once again hearing it. She responded with the same tone of voice he had used. Britton went back into the house and slammed the door.

When Bobbye finally came inside, there was a note on the kitchen table telling her that Britton wanted to talk to her about "something." The issue hung in the air and both of them knew what it was, but when the conversation finally started, it was important for both to avoid the old habits from the past and to identify exactly what had happened and what their feelings were concerning it.

Bobbye said that she resented the implied criticism of the question, as though she didn't know that the hose was on. Britton said that he resented her "overreaction" to his simple question. He said he thought maybe a pipe had broken.

Both were confident that theirs was the correct "interpretation," but both wanted to continue their close connection as a couple more than they wanted to be "right." They shared feelings, listened to each other's point of view, and decided that the fact that they were both hot and tired that morning had something to do with how easily they had slipped back into old habits.

Both learned from the experience. Bobbye learned that old habits of hearing criticism where none was intended could be a limited way to have a conversation and could predispose an attitude that might not be correct. Britton learned that questions might sometimes be open to more than one interpretation, and when questions are asked in a loud voice, seldom is there going to be a gentle resolution right away.

Both saw that old habits regarding anger could be amended in their relationship to a process much more likely to provide the resolution, equity, and good feelings that both wanted. Prevention of harsh words and actions was too late at that point but overcoming old habits and old methods of dealing with anger was a step in the right direction.

Couple Exercise

Think of a current conflict or disagreement you have with each other. Be specific about the topic as you begin. If the general subject is "household chores," for example, make sure you are specific about the chore you want to discuss. It is harder to get to a resolution if you are vague about complaints and subjects.

Acknowledge and state your feelings about the specific subject. Use "I" statements and ask your partner to say back to you what you said. When both of you understand, give the partner the opportunity to share feelings. Paraphrase those feelings back to your partner.

Discuss options for the resolution.

Chapter 14
Negotiation

Negotiation is the final stage of clearing up anger. Negotiation is used most effectively after a couple in a disagreement has worked through each step of the anger contract. The Maces suggest it as a method:

- Only after the conflict has been identified and both partners are sure they are talking about the same issue.
- Only after each person has shared his or her feelings and really listened to the feelings of the other person.
- Only after each has understood the other's point of view.

To try to move too soon to rational suggestions about options to end the conflict is more than likely to prevent a resolution that will last. Going through the steps in the anger contract may SEEM to be wasting time better used in getting to a resolution, but the end result of the quarrel is not just the resolution. *One important outcome of this system for handling anger is to provide a deeper understanding of each other. Growing the relationship is just as important as resolving the disagreement.*

"Understanding one another is more important for maintaining respect and connection than is solving every problem," says Dr. Scott Stanley of PREP. Understanding is one of the goals of this process for diffusing anger. Understanding builds the "us" for the couple in ways that produce hope and closeness. Understanding is more important than agreement.

David and Vera not only designed the anger contract; they not only demonstrated how it worked to audiences of all kinds; they proved its practical validity in the crucible of their own experience. The Maces never advocated anything that did not work for and in their own relationship. In fact, the organization they founded which they called the ACME had as its early slogan "Building Better Marriages Beginning with Our Own."

> ***David:*** Just taking the anger out of the conflict does not clear up the disagreement. The disagreement is still there. But it does enable you to negotiate more calmly the options you have. It moves you into a position to view your options and proceed.
>
> Too many couples don't realize in the heat of anger that they have any options. That is the tragedy of it. Find a realistic way to take out the anger, and the future instantly looks brighter.
>
> And there are three options. The first is *capitulation*. We don't mean coercive capitulation, which implies a force of one kind or another and is in close relationships always a negative thing because it is destructive to what you want most to achieve. We mean caring capitulation, and it is a good thing because it is a gift of love.
>
> Caring capitulation is the first option to consider in the process of negotiation. It is examining yourself and seeing that after you hear your partner's ideas and feelings, you can clear the whole thing up by going over to the partner's position. But for caring capitulation to work, it must be a two-way process.
>
> Vera: Yes, one partner can't always be the one to capitulate. Otherwise, you are probably engaging in a form of coercion or evasion, which will never lead to an amicable and healthy settlement of the issue. Caring capitulation just asks, Can I come all the way over to where you are, now that I understand your point of view? If I find that I can, it becomes a gift of love. If I find that I cannot, we must move to another option, and the discussion goes on.

Capitulation would not be used more than ten percent of the time. If it is selected as the love gift that it is, it is made without secret resentment or score-keeping. It is chosen merely because one partner understands fully the other's point of view and decides to agree with it. This can happen, but rarely.

David: The second option in negotiation happens when neither partner is willing or able to give an inch on a particular issue. Their decision is simply to agree to disagree. This is called *co-existence.*

It is one way to settle the issue, but it does suggest that this issue should be a limited choice. It does not create a fund of love and goodwill. It does not promote tolerance. Tolerance is NOT accepting the intolerable. Tolerance is keeping an open mind.

Working toward a common mind and a unity of spirit is a worthwhile couple goal, especially as couples grow and change over time and as they become able to work out more and more of their disagreements. Co-existence will not lead to that unity.

Vera: Here is an example of coexistence from our own experience. When my mother died, she left me some money that had been invested. It was not a big amount, and inflation had already eaten into the dividends. David knew about the investment, and since we had moved by then to the US, he thought it would be wise to bring the money over here.

I resisted that idea very strongly. I recognized that he was sensible and had good judgment, but I still resisted it for a variety of reasons. I thought in the first place that the money had been made by my father in England, and therefore it should stay in England. I wanted to put it to good use there. Also, I had a niece with a severely disabled daughter, and I thought I could help some way if the money was readily available to me in England.

Also, I wanted the freedom to do what I chose with what I regarded as MY money. It represented financial independence to me, and I needed that. I had independence when I was growing up, and that is what I still wanted. I also thought that if for any reason I had to go to England on short notice, which would be I could use some money without even discussing the matter with David.

I knew that in England they were taking out exorbitant taxes and that would not be true in the US, but I still wanted the money to remain in England.

David put his point of view very clearly and sensibly, as he usually does, but he finally came to see that emotionally this was a subject very important to me. He did not agree with it—and still doesn't—but on this one point we agreed to coexist.

David: I saw that it was important to her and that it was HER money. She understood that the balance was shrinking due to inflation, but she wanted the money to stay in England anyway. It was a small measure of financial independence, but it was important to her. So, coexistence was the negotiating option we chose.

Britton: Wasn't this really capitulation, going over to her side and agreeing to leave the money in England?

David: No, capitulation only happens when one abandons his own point of view. I still hold the point of view that this is a bad financial decision. But I also understand that from sentiment and a kind of patriotism, Vera wants this money to stay in England. This is coexistence because I am still of the opinion that this is not sensible.

Vera: And I know he is right. I admit it. But I still want the money there. It is important to me at an emotional level. Coexistence on this subject has kept us close and maintaining a verbal connection, but it is still coexistence. We simply agree to disagree.

Co-existence may be used with about the same ratio as capitulation, ten percent. Co-existence happens when both partners have their minds made up, and while they may understand how the other feels, they do not agree. Further discussion is unnecessary because the meaning of the facts involved in the issue is interpreted differently for each partner. There can be no common mind on this subject.

David: So, after the anger and heat have been taken out of the conflict, the couple moves the subject back to the level of a disagreement. There is no way to negotiate a sensible solution until the anger is gone. When the subject is once more at the level of a disagreement, then the negotiation process can begin.

And there is a third option, and it is the option most often used when a couple gets to the level of being able to discuss their disputed situation calmly and rationally. This is called *compromise*. Here the couple engages in bargaining or "horse-trading." Each discusses what each is willing to consider as an alternative outcome to the subject under dispute.

This is the most common option of negotiation, used probably ninety percent of the time as couples hammer out their wishes and desires, their needs and opinions, toward reaching a point where BOTH are satisfied with whatever decision they come to. When many options have been considered, the couple is now collaborating on what they will do. Collaboration moves the process to a decision.

We hope these three options are creative. But we believe that they are ways of helping couples come together after some adversarial experience—a way of healing and facing the future together. There is a vital difference between burying or avoiding a conflict and facing it together even if you cannot agree and you can only coexist. Conflicts avoided are only left to fester and create resentment. Finding a way to discuss the areas of disagreement opens up the future for even more creativity.

Later in the interview week, the Woods asked the Maces to negotiate a subject of disagreement in the style of compromise and collaboration. Here is what they said about the disputed subject of responding to requests and invitations of speaking engagements when they were supposedly in their retirement period:

> ***Vera:*** What I want to talk with you about is how to reduce the number of invitations you respond to with a "yes." What I want to talk about is our new phase of real retirement.
>
> ***David:*** Well, let's talk about that. How do you see it?
>
> ***Vera:*** I think first of all that it is harder for you than for me. I am a slow-moving person. I like a slow tempo; my preferred rhythm of daily life is slow. Second, I like traveling, and we have certainly done a lot of it throughout our marriage as we have wandered over the face of the earth. But what I like is having arrived. I don't like the act of getting from one place to another. And you do. You like traveling.
>
> ***David:*** Yes, I find it freeing and relaxing.
>
> ***Vera:*** And third, I find it very satisfying to be in a more narrow world with you. You have needed the bigger world of professional relationships, and as those have grown smaller, that has made retirement harder for you. It is not hard for me; I quite like our two-some having some time to ourselves.
>
> ***David:*** I don't mind saying "no" to the many requests I still receive. I know that I couldn't humanly accomplish all of them. No one could. And I don't mind the smaller world of retirement, but I don't take well, as you know, to the concept of older people being tended by someone, or playing shuffleboard and engaging in only small talk. I am not nearly as socialized as you are, and it is not a prospect that brings me joy to think about having to do.

Vera: I don't think we are going just yet to a place exclusively for a senior living. So, I don't want to talk about that eventuality. I want to talk about us, just us, right now.

David: I do welcome more time to listen to classical music, more time to read poetry, more time to re-read the classics of literature, and, of course, more time to just talk with you. I love talking with you about what we are reading, about our thoughts on the world situation, about our remembrances of cultures we have visited. You have a very active and original mind, and I love to engage with it.

Vera: I want us to continue to communicate with each other about our wants and needs. I know that they are not the same as they were three or four years ago, and I think it is important that we keep up-to-date with what each of us needs right now. We have always done that over the years, and I think it is important to do in retirement.

David: I do as well. We are in an exciting place of contemplating the rewarding and pleasurable things that each of us would like to do. Our lives have been extraordinarily rich and busy, and this is a new situation.

Just think of all the times we have been confronted with mammoth tasks, and we said to each other, "How will we ever accomplish that?" Then we got busy and began the preparations that would make the task possible. I think that is one of the goals of retirement for me. I want to keep busy with just enough tasks that it keeps the energy level up to keep going.

Vera: I think we are good at handling the big tasks and big situations. Take the recent request to come to Australia and speak. I just did not think I could handle it, and you and I discussed it. We negotiated a change in the time, and they put it off six months for us. That is an example of how we took the reality of retirement, health, and energy and made it work for us and for our relationship.

What I want for us is to negotiate on the small things, on the little things that keep coming and keep coming. Before we realize it, the list of all those small things we are being asked to do simply becomes overwhelming for both of us. Saying "yes" to a few small things leads in a very short time to more than either of can handle.

David: I hear you saying that all the many small requests we get to add up and rob us of time and energy. And I am the one who says "yes" to many of these because of the personal ties to the people asking. You are wanting us to discuss the small tasks as well as the big. Is that what you are saying?

Vera: Somewhat. I admit that I don't have the energy I used to. But I don't think you do either. I want to find some way that the pressure can be lifted from you. I see how tired you get from these tasks, and I would like us to find a way to preserve your energy as long as possible.

I share that pressure with you; I feel it. Some of these pressures just crowd in on you and I feel very deeply the inner fatigue that comes to you as you try to respond. And then when you are really fatigued, you and I don't get to have the talks and walks that we both enjoy. Reducing the pressures of saying yes to invitations would also give us more quality time together.

David: I know you feel deeply about this. What would be a solution satisfying to you? Would you want me to stop writing books and articles? Would you want me to stop going to major conferences where I meet old friends and colleagues? That would be one solution, but I would not feel good about that. The requests are an inevitable part of who we are and what we have done.

I am willing, as we talked about much earlier, to keep the number of requests within a manageable limit, but short of canceling obligations which we have already accepted, there isn't anything we can do right now. Or at least, that I am willing to do.

Vera: Another concern for me is that this kind of situation, where you continue to accept too many requests for involvement, is exactly what happened before you had your heart attacks. I am afraid that it is building up again and that there is not anything I can do about it. That time, nature intervened; nature relieved you of the pressures of work.

It was a traumatic time for me, and I'm sure it was for you. And I think it should not have to take a situation where you were near unto death in order to reduce the pressures of responding to the requests you receive. I want to help you with this. I want to help relieve the pressure.

David: Yes, I know you do. But I cannot take back some of the "yes" responses that I have already made. And I did discuss those events with you. I never make a commitment without discussing it with you. I am aware that some of these do put an overload on the calendar, but that is already done.

But let's start with next year's calendar. That is now completely clear. Let's look at it together. Together we will decide whether or not to put any responsibilities on it.

Vera: I already know of two trips that we are talking about for next year.

David: Yes, but they are not decided. And you have just as much power as I do. You can say what you want to do and what you don't. You are involved as much as I am with requests from dear friends to whom it is hard to turn down invitations.

I know that in the past I was more involved than you in the responses to invitations. But that is no longer true. You are now involved in saying "no." I will listen to your reasons for saying "no." If the reasons seem justified, I will abide by them. That also includes the invitations that are just to me, such as the medical school meetings or the pastoral care conferences.

Vera: But that puts me in the position of always being the negative one. And I don't want to be the one who always says "no."

David: But you are saying "no" so that you can say "yes" to giving us more time and more freedom. We will be claiming some of the time that each of us is saying we want. It will be a new kind of time management for us. That is what you really want, isn't it?

Vera: It's the creative use of "no." I could probably grow to like it, but it is a delicate situation. I don't want to be manipulative.

David: I don't feel manipulated. I think your motivation is that you are helping us by helping me cut back on the schedule. I feel appreciative of your efforts, and I sometimes need you to be sensitive to my energy level, especially when all our lives I have been the one to overload our schedule.

I don't feel that you are being negative, and I don't think that you are being manipulative. You can help me by speaking up.

Vera: Hmmm. Speaking the truth in love.

David: Yes, I think so. And I must be ready to have you act firmly on behalf of both of us. This has happened before, you know. I heard you about Australia and that worked out well.

Vera: Yes, you did. And I was very pleased about that.

David: So, you need to be more assertive about this new arrangement. I want you to take a more definite role in what we say "yes" to. I will share all of our requests and invitations with you, and you can choose what you think the both of us can handle. I know that you will be fair. I hear your concerns.

Vera: Thank you. That relieves my mind of some of the worries I have had about retirement and how to be sure that it is a pleasure for both of us and more relaxing and healthful. Britton and Bobbye, I am aware that we have taken a great deal of time with it, I'm afraid, but it is something important.

Bobbye: It certainly is. It is where most people are going to be eventually. And it gives a great model about how the concerns and hopes of both partners can be expressed about a very realistic subject.

Also, both of you have been talking about time management, and that is a relevant subject whether a person is in retirement or in the first year of marriage. We live in a fast-paced world, with cultural demands on everybody's time. I think the terms of this discussion are essential, as you both laid out your ideas, fears, feelings, and concerns and reached a decision that you both can live with. It was beautiful to listen to.

Britton: Everyone battles the demands of time. And that is especially true for couples who are trying to carve out some time for themselves. If both husband and wife are working at something that is meaningful to them, if there are children in the home, if there is community involvement as well, it's going to cause some pressures as they try to have couple time.

You two have given an excellent example of a fair way to negotiate a compromise on a subject of great concern. Thank you both.

Michelle and the late Joe Hernandez of the Family Wellness program echo the Maces' negotiation suggestions at the point of compromise or collaboration. After the heat of the conflict has been moved back to the level of a disagreement and the couple is better able to discuss the subject calmly, they make a list together off all the viable options they have to settle the dispute. It should be done quickly, with a minimum of analysis and no effort to evaluate. The options should be numerous—some of them might even be humorous or wildly impractical. But even if the couple has to stop to laugh, they both know that it is a serious list.

The list is an experiment designed to respect each partner's preferences and ideas. It is meant to value the "us," the relationship. Instead of dividing them on a particular subject, they are now working together on this task as a couple team. Together they choose one of the options or parts of several. Together they analyze and evaluate.

The Hernandezes also recommend that the couple set an appointment to meet again on a given date for the purpose of reviewing the compromise solution that they chose. Depending on the details of the option they chose, the appointment might be within a few days. It might need to be months away.

But at that time if the option is no longer satisfactory to both, or one partner has failed to keep his or her part of it in the way he or she agreed to do, the subject needs to be addressed again, with other options considered and implemented. Another appointment date is set just to make sure that both are still pleased with their choices.

In this style of coming to a workable option, a compromise appears to take a long time, and that is probably true, but it also allows for the opinions, personalities, preferences, and choices of both partners to be honored. Even engaging in it says loudly that both partners matter; it is a safe and interesting way for each to learn more about themselves and about their partner.

In order for negotiation to work, it has to be fair and equitable, just and honest. Both negotiators must be present and willing. Whether it is a couple, a corporation, or a country doing the negotiating, the same rules apply. Because disagreements are a part of living, finding a way to work through them that respects both sides is crucial.

Some couples have so many areas of disagreement in their relationship that they consider off-limits even for discussion, that their daily commerce together is like a floor of a room that is full of dirty clothes, excess furniture, and boxes of unpacked books. There is no longer freedom or safety even to walk around in the room. Not for the couple, not for the family, and not for guests who come to call.

Using a successful (and sometimes a new) method for clearing up disputed couple issues can immediately brighten the future for both persons. When both partners feel listened to and respected, they are more willing to consider change and more open to surprising new perspectives. THE FUTURE IS NOT JUST THE SUM OF THINGS PAST AND THINGS PRESENT.

The Woods' Experience with Negotiation

Britton and Bobbye married in 1956 under one contract of home duties and who would do them. The contract was modeled on the traditions of the times and the habits of the homes they had grown up in. In the middle years of their marriage as both had jobs and many volunteer duties, they tried to change who would perform some of those duties. Their MEG frequently heard about the difficulties of that change, particularly regarding who was going to be responsible for washing, starching, and ironing Britton's dress shirts.

For years, Bobbye had performed this task, but when she completed her graduate work and began to teach full time, she wanted a change. Britton liked to wear a different shirt every day, so when the situation really needed to be addressed, there were several shirts needing laundering and ironing. Something had to be done.

Working through their Anger Agreement brought out many feelings and suggestions concerning what might be done. Bobbye suggested buying more shirts; Britton said that was too expensive. Bobbye suggested leaving off the starching; Britton said he liked the finish starch provided.

Finally, their discussion reached the point of negotiation: Bobbye would continue to do the family laundry, as she had done before, but the shirts would go to the dry cleaners, where they would be professionally washed, starched, and ironed, just as Britton liked them. It looked like a workable option, but the issue was not finished.

The problem was that the compromise did not specifically state who would take the shirts to the laundry. The shirts stacked up, with each partner expecting the other to fulfill that responsibility. Finally, one morning the shirts appeared in the doorway to the Woods' bedroom, bundled into a big pile. Bobbye left them there, and this was a conversation at breakfast:

Britton: My shirts need to go to the cleaners to be laundered.

Bobbye: Perhaps you could take them this morning.

Britton: Or you could take them on your way to work when you take your other dry cleaning.

Bobbye: I am not going by the cleaners this morning. I have no dry cleaning to take.

Britton: I am running out of clean shirts.

Bobbye: I am sorry about that. I can wash them this afternoon after I get home from school. But I am not ironing them. And they are YOUR shirts.

(a long pause)

Britton: OK. I'll take them.

Expectations concerning roles and household duties often lead to the Anger Agreement and ultimately to negotiation. But when couples are honest with each other and take the recommended steps, change is possible and the old gives way to the new. Their MEG had a party when this issue was settled.

A Couple Exercise

Choose one routine household task on which the two of you do not have the same opinion.

Each partner shares answers to the following:

1. Name the household task.
2. Describe what is needed in the performance of this task.
3. How do you wish it could be handled differently?
4. Suggest what your next steps might be.

Chapter 15

The Family and Anger

The preservation and protection of the family have been a goal throughout history. Raising healthy children fully equipped to take their place in society with confidence was once an honored and profitable occupation.

One of the tragedies of modern life has been the number of cracks weakening the family structure, as divorce, abuse, abandonment, drugs, and poverty takes a toll. To have some kind of security that being in a relationship offers and to avoid the issues of a legal commitment, some couples drift in and out of cohabitation.

These tangled alliances further weaken the family structure and subject the children involved to much unnecessary pain and suffering. In fact, the children in many of those fragile relationships are often uncertain as to their family identity, since sometimes they are a blend of other relationships and other unions, now no longer functioning in any parental way. They merely become a part of a group of children from a variety of sources, and only a small number of the lucky ones avoid the dismal statistics of being locked into poverty and a future pock-marked with the detritus left by gangs, drugs, and risky behavior.

As the cracks widen in the family structure, many grandparents now are raising their grandchildren. Due to serious parental disregard for the importance of family to the broader society, children are left to be farmed out to some willing relative. The family is not yet in full-blown crisis, but the cracks need to be repaired soon.

Quite often, the underlying issue in the dissolution of the family is the unresolved anger of one or both partners. Learning to use a method for dealing with anger that honors the feelings of BOTH can be an aid to healing old hurts, as well as providing a greater understanding of current issues.

At the very least it offers children needed security and safety. At the best, it offers them a model for the future that provides them a better and more stable cultural environment.

Very early in their careers, the Maces saw that conflict, unaddressed and unresolved, could affect both the couple and the extended family. Their research was drawn from cultures around the world, as well as studies into how couples dealt with divisive issues. The figures in the three styles of marital relationships reflect their findings.

THREE STYLES OF MARITAL RELATIONSHIPS

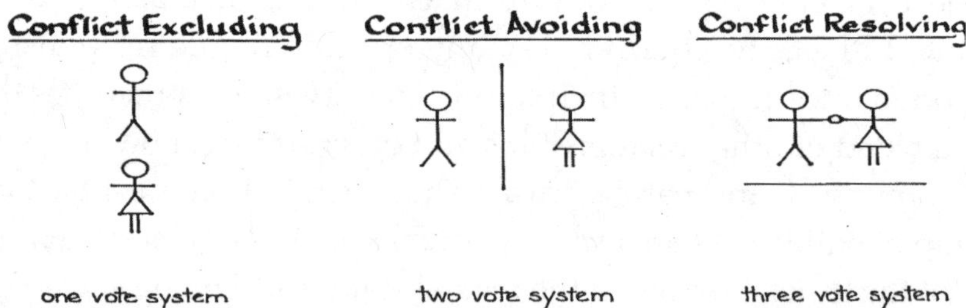

The most common pattern around the world that the Maces found was what they labeled a one-vote system. In the Conflict-excluding style, one person (usually the male) has the final say, the vote, about what will happen regarding conflict and its outcome.

In this system, the female agrees to be in the one-down position, usually in exchange for being taken care of but sometimes merely to avoid violence or bitter arguments.

In some cultures, the male is considered superior due to tradition and to the fact that he makes more money. In other cultures, the joke is that the man may be the titular "head" of the household, but the woman is the "neck." This suggests that the woman must use circuitous and conniving methods to be heard in her own household (to turn that "head" in the way she wants it to go), but those methods are not used in public perception.

In this Conflict-excluding model, there is no shared power and rarely closeness, or intimacy. Conflict may have been excluded, but the one-up position of one partner suggests that there may be many under-the-surface manipulations going on that make the homelife less than smooth. The female has very little status and looks to her spouse for any major decision that affects the family.

The effect on the family of the one-vote system for handling conflict is that children growing up in that home see no model of adults working through a disagreement together. If the father has the vote, sons can grow up expecting women to have little or no voice on issues of disagreement. The male is "naturally" to be in charge. Daughters growing up in that system can work for years to claim their own vote and to do so responsibly and without duplicity.

A second pattern, the Conflict-avoiding style, developed after WWII. More women at this time went into the workplace and had an income. This set them up to want a more democratic formula in their families, a vote for the husband and a vote for the wife.

In the two-vote system, husband and wife roles for accomplishing all tasks were assigned to each partner. If something did not get done (or not done well or on time), both partners knew who to blame. The conflict was largely avoided by each partner accomplishing their agreed-upon tasks. Roles and jobs were the emphasis, with a line in the figure between the couple suggesting that although conflict might be avoided, so was any real intimacy.

The effect on the family of the two-vote system can be that children raised in this environment value efficiency above any other quality. They believe that personal accomplishment outweighs cooperation and collaboration. Intimacy is not valued as highly as responsibility. Independence is encouraged in this family style; sharing of feelings and ideas is not. High achievement is rewarded; communicating hopes and wishes is not.

The third figure shows the Conflict-resolving three-vote system. This means that in the time of a disagreement, the husband gets a vote, the wife gets a vote, and the relationship itself gets a vote. How does the relationship cast its vote, you might ask. This happens when both partners value their relationship more than being "right" about an issue and are willing to measure the effect of the disagreement on the relationship, the "us." This happens when the couple designs a way to settle disagreements that allows negotiation and mutual efforts toward reconciliation.

Both partners value intimacy, closeness, understanding, and growth; this is indicated by the postures of the figures. In the three-vote model, they stand together on a firm foundation. They hold hands and regard the divisive issue as an obstacle for their couple-team to get over, around, or through. They have found the resources to work through their issue, such as some form of the Anger Contract, and they use it.

They work together as a team, when conflicts arise, and they demonstrate that they regard themselves as competent to handle the issues that come to them. The effect on children in the family of the three-vote system is that they grow up seeing how adults can admit their anger and yet work out a resolution to the conflict that is fair and equitable.

All around the world, the Maces taught the advantages of the three-vote-system for the family structure. They were concerned about the effects of anger on that structure. Having in place a formula for resolving conflict and choosing to use it at moments of stress and tensions enriches everyone involved. It is a useful "tool" that helps build productive families who have learned skills for handling their own anger and disagreements.

It was part of what the Maces meant when they spoke of a peaceful world being founded on peace in the home.

Bobbye: What about couples fighting in the presence of their children? Wouldn't that be a difficult thing, even if they later make up and life goes on?

David: Yes, I think it is a difficulty. Young children think that a conflict which they witness their parents having is going to lead to a divorce. They have friends whose parents split up over repeated conflicts. They have nightmares about it. They are hyper-sensitive to it.

Bobbye: Then how could the conflict be turned toward growth? How could the children benefit from a fight?

David: There is no benefit to witnessing a fight between parents when one or both are demonstrating Anger-as-Power and refusing to move the conflict to a level where there can be a discussion of the issue and negotiation. In fact, as I said, this can be difficult and unfortunately that can be carried on into the future, as the child grows up to imitate the destructive power he saw one or both of his parents wielding.

But the benefits are there if the conflict is handled correctly, because, you see, the child also gets angry. And to see the parents angry about a certain subject but dealing with it and trying to work it out teaches a valuable lesson to the child.

The child sees the negative emotions and also feels their power, but he also sees the parents dealing with those emotions and arriving at some kind of workable solution.

I do not think it is helpful for children to see their parents fighting if there is some kind of attack by one or both of them. But it IS helpful to see them acknowledge their emotions, state to each other that they are angry, and still work toward a reasonable and mutually satisfying resolution. Then the child sees that when he is angry, it is OK to say so.

In fact, he sees that it is very good to acknowledge the anger, but not good to attack the other person. He sees that it is not a helpful part of the process to deny or to conceal anger.

What he sees is a way to USE anger in order to arrive at a process that can please the persons involved. *It is a valuable lesson and he has learned that lesson from his parents.*

Britton: You are giving the child the equipment to use himself in stressful or angry situations. There is no better person to give a child this equipment than the parent. It is truly a life lesson.

It is a kind of parent-effectiveness just as negotiation itself is a useful skill to teach our children. I have three daughters, and negotiation about mowing the lawn is something I do with them. I have grass allergies which make mowing the lawn uncomfortable for me.

I worked out a deal with one of my daughters about lawn mowing. They will look at the grass in the backyard and say it looks like about a $10 job. I look at the grass and say it looks like about a $5 job. Then we end up somewhere in between. I think it is healthy to teach them this process. A negotiating tool is useful as they grow up.

Bobbye: Yes, but you are talking about negotiating a price for a piece of work about which there is no disagreement and no anger.

David: That is why you have to take the anger out of the conflict before you can de-escalate the issue back to the level of a disagreement. The disagreement is the only place where you have a chance at negotiation. And when children watch this process taking place in their presence, they are learning a process that will serve them well in their future lives. Fights are never a happy experience, but they can have a benefit.

In fact, turning our arguments as parents into lessons for how to deal with anger is one way to enrich the family. Children who grow up in households who show only an ineffective way to resolve a troubling issue are usually children unable to handle their own strong emotions in adulthood.

Clearing up anger by using the Anger Contract is one way to help the family cope with issues that can cripple family growth and harmony. It is really an important teaching tool that parents can use.

Very few relationships manage to stay balanced and peaceful all the time. But those who successfully resolve their disagreements are those most likely to stay friends and lovers throughout their lives together. And those who stay friends and lovers throughout their lives are those who have the greatest positive impact on their families.

The Woods' Experience with Anger and the Family

One late afternoon, Bobbye and Britton sat around their kitchen table with their three daughters in their new house in a new city. The two older daughters had come home from their respective colleges for the weekend just to see the new house, and one of them was very angry.

That daughter told her parents that for two days previously she had tried to call home and learned that the telephone was "not a working number." She felt confused and abandoned, she said. She thought that it meant her parents did not care what was happening to her and probably never had.

At this point, her sisters wanted to chime in with similar concerns, but Britton told them this was the time just to listen to only one person. Even when the angry daughter delivered her stinging criticism, cried, and got up to leave the table, Britton got up too, put his arm around her, brought her back to the table, and assured her that the family wanted to hear all her feelings.

Bobbye and Britton did not tell her that she was being disrespectful to her tuition-paying parents. She was not ready to handle that. They just kept listening. Finally, she said that the reason she had been calling was that she was thinking of changing colleges. She was not sure if all her courses would count in her declared major, and she didn't know if they had her same sorority. The whole issue was making her very upset and she had needed her parents' counsel on the subject. When her home telephone number did not work, it was the last straw.

Both parents told her that being scared about the future was understandable. They gave some parental advice about how she could answer some of the questions that were concerning her. They commended her for including them in her decision-making. Privately they were relieved that THEY were not the issue after all, but they did not say that.

At that point (when ALL the feelings were heard and acknowledged), she also had room to hear about the move, about bridge loans, mortgages, and days without a telephone. She was even able to hear her little sister's humorous story about moving the cat and two dogs in her car when earlier she was not interested in that story. Now there was room for affectionate hugs and other family news.

All families are going to have disruptive scenes that can wound and confuse. There is no realistic way to avoid them. But when those families also have a way to process the anger and high feeling that are a part of those scenes, they have a way to restore harmony to the family and a model for the future.

Couple Exercise

In the blank preceding the following statements, indicate your opinion. When completed, discuss your choices with your partner.

SA (strongly agree), A (agree), D (disagree), or SD (strongly disagree):

1. _____ My partner and I need to find a better way to process anger.
2. _____ We seldom share our feelings in an argument.
3. _____ We sometimes attack each other with words when we are angry.
4. _____ I tend to withdraw when we are arguing.
5. _____ I feel powerless when my partner is angry.
6. _____ My partner often misunderstands my point of view.
7. _____ We never argue in front of our family.
8. _____ I would rather win an argument than listen to my partner's ideas.

Chapter 16
Anger, Sex, and Intimacy

Intimacy is composed of many facets: kisses, pats, special looks, gestures, secrets, words of endearment, cuddles, shared memories of loving behaviors and shared conversations, to name only a few. Reducing the word intimacy to mean sexual intercourse alone is a short-sighted approach—although a common one—and puts undue stress on a couple as time, medications, surgeries, and other health issues can become a factor in its sexual activity.

An overlooked impact on a couple's intimacy quotient is how it handles anger. If the couple's difficult and divisive issues remain unaddressed and simmering under the surface, the closeness and joy that could be theirs are often affected. In fact, it is never too late to set an appointment regarding an issue, share feelings about it with each other and paraphrase those feelings, and discuss the options together concerning what you might do to resolve the issue.

Like someone holding a beach ball underwater so that no one will know it is there, anger unresolved drains energy, keeps the person from interacting in a pleasant way with others, and prevents his or her playful engagement on the beach of life. Even if someone were drowning, the person holding the beach ball under water would be unable to give help. Anger has a way of pre-occupying our thoughts and weighing on our bodies.

Choosing a responsible way to handle and resolve our quarrels is a practical way to keep intimacy flourishing and sexual relations perennially exciting—the one area that no healthy, growing couple can do without.

Here is what the Maces believe about sex and intimacy and how to increase the pleasure of both.

Britton: How do you see anger connecting to the subject of sex?

David: Anger has a much more disruptive impact on the relationship than sexual difficulties. Sex is a function of the love relationship, and if the love relationship is all right, people can usually find a way of meeting each other's sexual needs. But if they practice anger-as power on each other, if they can't deal with anger constructively, if they hold on to every grievance, then sex eventually becomes disconnected from the whole state of intimacy. There may be physical closeness up to a certain point if they continue to live together, but there is no growing emotional connection.

Bobbye: I can't understand how disassociating sex from any kind of emotional closeness produces a good effect.

David: Yes, I heard someone say recently that *sex without a loving relationship is like a diploma without an education*. That's well put, isn't it?

Bobbye: It is. What are some of your ideas about sex and a loving relationship?

David: I think that sex is a relatively minor part of a loving relationship, although an important part. But just think of the time it takes up. Someone has recently done a time study of sex over the course of a year. In the study, you see that sex takes up very little time, just a weekend in the unfolding of a whole year. And putting it into a proportion of time, I think it is indicative of the fact that we've given it far too much emphasis. If we could concentrate on communication, for example, and clear up misunderstandings for couples, they could more easily find ways to meet each other's needs sexually.

Britton: What about people who change partners often for sex? What effect would it have on them to be operating in this pattern?

David: I think it's not what effect this pattern has on them, but rather why they choose this pattern. This series of episodes—of one-night stands—can provide a kind of pseudo-intimacy. Then it releases that person from the need to do the things that provide a deeper sense of intimacy.

Quite possibly what happens to these people is that when the superficial expressions of excitement and novelty begin to wear out, and they begin to confront each other at deeper levels, they have to run away from each other and start all over again with somebody else at the superficial level. They continue to choose this pattern because it's all they know about intimacy. And in choosing it, they are blocking out the very things that could produce and sustain real intimacy.

Some even have children together, but without choosing to explore the things that can create real intimacy, they will eventually drift apart and move on to someone else. All the new and emerging statistics about co-habitation bear this out. Those who continue to change partners and move in and out of sexual relationships are failing to find the one thing that could anchor them in the world and give them a stronger sense of identity.

The point is that marriage is a fluid and flexible process, which can never really be stable. Marriage is adaptation; marriage is change and growth. Marriage moves toward objectives but never completely arrives because the objectives themselves change. Movement and change are the nature of life, including marriage, and to really grow in intimacy, a couple must be open to that fact. And growth in intimacy takes time; it is a condition that cannot be achieved quickly.

Regarding the people who have only short-term relationships with each other, they are denying themselves the opportunity to experience the intimacy that only grows over time together, as a couple meets the change that is a part of life. Our bodies can meet, they are saying by their actions, but our minds must not meet.

Britton: How do you deal with sex within the groups that you lead?

David: The sexual relationship is an adjustment area. However, there has been so much good work done in this area, that we have chosen to put the emphasis on the love relationship. We are not saying that sex will take care of itself on all occasions, but we do think it will in most.

All this information about sex and sexual performance in the media is in some instances causing anxiety about sex, which didn't exist before. What Vera and I are trying to do is soft-pedal the emphasis on performance of the sexual act itself and instead focus on healthy ways of communication for couples and ways to deal with the important subjects that they want to talk about.

In fact, *we have found that adjustment areas such as sex, money, parenting, or in-laws take care of themselves very largely when the couple has a commitment to growth, an effective communication system, and a successful way of dealing with their disagreements.*

Britton: Do you see sex as a part of communication?

David: Yes, but no more important than many other subjects that couples have to deal with. What we do is give them the skills and tools and insights to make the adjustments for themselves in their own way.

Bobbye: So, you see sex as only one area of communication, and isolating it may produce feelings of anxiety about it. It is a part of a couple adjustment, but only a part.

David: Yes, there are a number of areas about sex that can lead to difficulties, especially the effects of time and pharmaceuticals, but they all boil down to one main area—and that is about performance. The sexual act is something perfectly natural, but you foul it up if you focus too much attention on performance. Part of you is happily functioning, and part of you is looking to see if you are doing it right and if you can improve. It can spoil the whole effect when we are anxiously focusing on the performance.

Measuring and studying our performance paralyzes the freedom of spontaneity. What is needed is a candid discussion by both partners so that any difficulties or reservations can be dealt with and understood by both.

Vera: And in our work with groups, when the subject of sex comes up, we simply treat it like any other area of adjustment. We are quite plain about it, and if it does not come up, we do not deal with it, just as we would not discuss money or time-management if couples are not interested.

David: Yes, some people show films on sex to create a discussion in a group, but we feel that emphasizing the tools on communication and growth and dealing with anger is the best way to proceed. Then couples who want to discuss sex have a way to do it without undue emphasis. If you show a film, immediately you are treating sex as something different and it automatically produces anxiety, especially in those who are concerned about performance. When it does come up, the group is usually surprised to find how easy it is to talk about.

Britton: Could it be that the couples attending the Marriage Enrichment seminars are placing the subject of sex as a part of the whole marriage relationship and not themselves isolating it as something special and apart from the whole?

David: Absolutely. Sex belongs as an integral part of the whole developing couple relationship, and most healthy couples see it that way. We have found that once couples have a way to talk to one another that builds a sense of safety and understanding, any subject can be approached with an attitude of confidence. *The key to intimacy, as I have said many times, is developing a way to process anger and clear up its effects.* When that has been done, the couple is free to approach other areas of adjustment that need to be discussed, such as sex and intimacy.

Anger, unchecked and unchanneled, can also have a strong effect on the intimacy and tenderness couples need to experience every day with each other. Here is a conversation about anger, growth, and tenderness between David and Vera.

David: Does dealing with the issues that arise and cause conflict produce tenderness? The answer is no. But *dealing with divisive issues clears away the rabid weed that is anger, which destroys the places where tenderness grows.*

It's almost as if you were growing an exotic flower in your garden, and you were not sure it was going to come up. You've got to keep the weeds away from it because they could overwhelm it and steal the nutrients in the soil. You must deal with the angry situations as they come up—and you must not use anger as a weapon or as a badge of power. In order to clear out a place for the flower, the sweet tenderness, to bloom, you have to find mutually helpful ways to deal with anger. When you reduce the number of toxic situations by clearing them up, you are giving tenderness a chance.

Vera: Are you saying that you and I were not tender before we chose a new way to handle anger?

David: Yes, we were. At least you were. You had the willingness and the ability. But it wasn't until I got my anger dealt with that I could really be free to be tender with you. In practice, at least in terms of the impact, *the emotion of love and the emotion of hostility cannot coexist over time.*

Hostility and anger will trample all efforts to harbor tender and gentle feelings. Anger unacknowledged and unaddressed has about the same effect on a relationship as an affair—wounds, lack of trust, and distance. *Clearing up anger brings a new shine to the relationship and makes possible all kinds of intimacies.*

The Woods' Experience with Anger, Sex, and Intimacy

In life, love, and close relationships, the way issues of anger are handled (or not handled) often cast long shadows into the future. What goes around comes around, as the saying goes.

That is how Pastor Ryon Price began his sermon one Sunday morning. He told the congregation the story of a businessman who rode the bus to work every morning. The businessman noticed that very often there was a panhandler who solicited money from the bus's passengers.

One Friday morning, the panhandler approached the businessman and was given $10. The businessman also told him, "Never Despair."

On Monday morning, the panhandler met the businessman at the door of the bus and handed him $10. Then he gave him another $10. "What is this for?" asked the puzzled businessman. "Never Despair won the big horserace Saturday afternoon and paid off 5 to 1," he answered. "This is your share." What goes around comes around, said Pastor Price.

Bobbye and Britton within a recent time period tackled the subject of intimate touch, which over the years and over significant prostate issues had led to some troubling misconceptions and even hard feelings. Concentrating on one misunderstanding and one false assumption at a time, they were finally able to reach a new comprehension toward each other's bodies.

Bobbye and Britton then remembered hearing a sex therapist who declared that no couple really understood intimacy until they had been married for five or six decades. It takes time to discuss important areas of sex and intimacy, but that discussion can lead to many discoveries concerning how to best deal with the satisfaction level of both partners.

Clearing up the misunderstandings toward touch that each had harbored toward the other (without ever discussing them) began to bring back the enthusiasm, the freedom, and the spontaneity of the earliest years of marriage. Several friends now refer to Britton and Bobbye as "the love-birds," and family members laughingly joke about putting the grandparents in the back seat of the car on trips so that they can "smooch." What goes around comes around.

Reducing the effects of anger and hostility by a frank, open, and honest conversation about feelings and points of view is using that "tool" to recapture some of the physical joys of intimacy that many couples fear are gone with youth.

Couple Exercise

Discuss together the following questions:

1. What is a characteristic about your partner that you especially value?
2. What was one of your favorite vacations together and why?
3. What are some of the favorite body parts of your partner?
4. What is a subject that might need some clarity of discussion within your relationship? If this is not a good time to discuss that subject, set an appointment for a more convenient time. Keep the appointment. Give each partner plenty of time to disclose feelings and attitudes toward that subject.
5. What is one facet of your relationship that pleases you?

From This Point On

Bobbye and Britton were invited to share information they deemed important regarding marriage with the congregation of an African Baptist Church in Dallas, Texas. The members of the congregation had come to America from various African countries. The Woods shared the three strengths (The Primary Coping System) that they had learned and practiced from the Maçes, but with a concentration that day on communication.

When they completed their presentation and sat down, the pastor immediately got up and with a loud voice asked, "Was this American?" The people shouted, "No!" The pastor asked again, "Was this American?" The people once again shouted, "No!" Sitting alone on a front pew, the Woods began to worry that what they had said might be about to stir up some kind of international incident. They had no idea where this was going.

The pastor then said to the congregation, "No, this was international!" He then explained to Bobbye and Britton, "If you had shared with us how you do family and relate as Americans, we would not have listened. That is because we have observed the ineffective ways many Americans relate to each other as families. What you said could be said around the world, and we believe it is how families in many cultures should talk to each other."

This validates once again the Maces as marriage pioneers. Their studies of some seventy-nine different cultures not only gave them insights into the many ways that marriage works around the world but also allowed them to introduce the Coping System and prove how it could aid couple relationships no matter the place or time. *The Maces were pioneers in the field of marriage education, but their practical ideas continue to be internationally relevant today.*

So, what are our recommendations to couples from this point on?

1. *Mutually commit to behavioral growth and change in your relationship.* Mutually decide what you most want to accomplish both in your individual lives and in your marriage. Commit to making it happen. Commitment adds structure, team-building, and excitement to your relationship.

In an online article celebrating a significant drop in the divorce rates in the UK after decades of hovering around fifty percent, it was reported that the divorce rate of those married less than three years fell to thirty-nine percent, those married for over five years fell to thirty-five percent, and those married even longer fell to a whopping thirty percent. This is indeed good news for the families torn apart by the issues of divorce.

Researchers into the reasons for the substantial drop discovered that "men particularly who make a clear decision to commit are more likely to be happy and stable." Women, who file for divorce twice as often as men, suddenly have slowed the dissolution of the marital relationship and proclaim themselves as more willing to "work on the marriage."

A mutual commitment to growth can be the "door" to exciting possibilities for couples over time to stay with both friends and lovers.

2. *Mutually develop an effective communication system, a way of talking to each other that is both honest and encouraging.* How you talk and listen matters. Add a talk time every day that

is private and self-revealing. Communication is the practical "tool" that lets those who matter to us both know us and know best how we would like to be loved. An intimate talk time every day is where couples articulate to each other the goals they would like to achieve, both for themselves and for their relationship. The more honest and encouraging the talk time, the greater the growth of the relationship.

A growing body of research both in the field of psychology and the field of health care suggests that a thoughtful conversation with a spouse can not only increase intimacy but improve health "in meaningful and lasting ways." When partners share positive conversations and share them often, depression lessens, falling asleep gets easier, and even the common cold is over sooner. Researchers found that honest and encouraging conversations between responsive partners are "linked to better overall health."

3. *Mutually design a way to deal creatively with the inevitable conflict and anger generated by the sharing of life in depth.* Be creative. The process must fit for both partners. Using faithfully the process you design is important for ultimate success. Repeated anger and unresolved conflicts can destroy progress achieved in growth and rewarding conversation. This is the "tool" that can reveal the most immediate progress in a closer and growing relationship.

Couples who learn these three timeless strengths need to find ways to practice it in front of their children. The children can then grow up confident that they know how to relate and grow their own relationships with others. Schools would be wise to educate their students with skills that promote healthy relationships and thus counteract bullying, gangs, and isolation.

When you make a *mutual commitment to growth,* it takes both partners; that is why the Maces used the word "mutual." Of course, one partner may be more committed than the other, and good things can begin to happen. But both points of view toward relationship are necessary, and both assessments of what can happen together help make the desired goals more likely to be reached.

One person, for example, may look at a page of sheet music and say it is a paper with lines, dots, and circles. And that person would be right. Another person could look at the same page and say it is a famous Chopin Etude with an exceptionally beautiful melody. And that person would be right. In health and growth, there is no ONE point of view that is correct. In health and growth, both partners need to be involved and both need to take responsibility for that involvement, for their own opinions, and for the way they honor the point of view of the other.

Goals matter in life and marriage; otherwise, we are just allowing things to happen to us out of chance and circumstance. Just as smart citizens are encouraged to plan for their retirement, no matter what other expenses they have to meet currently, smart partners are those who envision an ideal they want to accomplish and plan for it. That mutual sharing regarding the "vision" they see for their future together and the mutual planning for how to achieve the "vision" is the key to making it happen.

Going through the "door" of *mutual commitment to growth* is an adventure, and every couple needs its own unique resources, both individually and relationally. Everyone is a pioneer in the marital adventure, but some information makes the adventure safer and more enjoyable for both persons.

The Maces at first believed that most couples just need specific information about how to get to a secure level of marriage enjoyment and heartfelt intimacy. Then they can take the information and safely make the marital adventure. However, by mid-career, the Maces had to admit that many couples would prefer to take the information, use it haphazardly, and make a few changes here and there. The couples never went far enough into the adventure of growth to experience the immense joys of couple intimacy.

Those couples chose only to "maintain" the *status quo* of their relationship, to keep it together and do only what was necessary to keep it from breaking apart. "Maintaining" is responsible; it is needed; it is commendable. If there are children in the home, they will someday thank you for the stable environment of safety and security that "maintenance" provided them as they grew up.

"Maintenance" of the status quo is not the same thing as working toward making each other happy by supporting the exact goals each is trying to achieve. It is not the same as designing couple-goals together and working toward making them come true. It is not the same as creating and enjoying the custom-made marriage. Dutifully and responsibly "maintaining" the marriage is not the same as a mutual commitment to growth. A mutual commitment to growth encourages progress for the "you," the "me," and the all-important "us." One partner can do "maintenance"; it takes both partners to make a mutual commitment.

Learning to talk to each other in a way that leads to understanding is a "tool" for growth. Several years ago, Bobbye and Britton worked for a month in an international church in Madrid, Spain, teaching marriage education. There they encountered many couples who had come from other countries to work or study in Spain. Some of these couples had fallen in love, married, and started to raise a family while struggling with the difficult issue of holding daily conversations in two different languages.

Theirs was the unique issue of having one birth language (or "language of the heart," as they called it), learning another language in order to study or work in Spain, and marrying someone who has a third language. Often, there was even a fourth language involved, English, which was spoken at the church and regarded as an international language.

Learning to relate to each other as a couple while integrating traditions, food, music, religion, and of course language was an exciting but often frustrating experience. Some of the couples did not like the taste of their partner's preferred cultural food, and often they bought groceries separately and prepared their food separately. In spite of this difference, all the couples spoke of integrating language as one of the most difficult tasks they faced.

Although most couples will not have to face conditions as dramatic as this, they all must negotiate the minefields of having different backstories, different educations, and different experiences in growing up. Some couples must even face the differences of an earlier relationship with someone else that often had its own special "language" of words to say and words NOT to say because of special meanings to one person. Putting differences together into a new "us" can be a formidable experience, since sometimes couples are in the middle of a divisive and sometimes hostile situation before they even realize it is a "situation."

Holding frequent honest conversations about where you are and what you want (not just what you don't want) is one way:

- *to smooth out the differences between you and*
- *to establish boundaries that help define the couple you want to be.*

Those conversations position both partners on their life journeys and are invaluable in giving the information that makes day-to-day interaction easier. This is one reason why the Maces referred to communication as a handy "tool," rather like a hammer, a battery-powered screwdriver, or a tape-measure for householders who need to fix something.

The Daily Sharing Time

One of the most helpful kinds of communication the Maces called the Daily Sharing Time. It is a process now recommended by today's marriage educators and counselors, and no matter what it is called by different marriage education programs, it is a necessary part of staying current and connected with the partner. *The Daily Sharing Time builds intimacy, contributes personal knowledge, and, like a GPS, shows where we have been, where we are, and where we want to go.*

This kind of conversation is what Bloody Mary in the musical "South Pacific" called "Happy Talk." Bloody Mary lived on Bali Hai, a beautiful south sea island caught up in the danger of WWII. Trying to survive the ravages of daily battles between the American and the Japanese navies, Bloody Mary encouraged her daughter and the American lieutenant who has fallen in love with her to use a "talk time"every day just to keep life bearable and in perspective.

When the two lovers inquired about the structure of this conversation, she told them to "talk about things you'd like to do," as well as places you would like to go. She advised sharing their dreams for the future with each other. If you don't know what you want, she told them, you won't be happy, even when your "dreams come true."

Bloody Mary was a realist. She knew exactly what kind of difficult world she lived in and exactly what odds she and her daughter faced every day just to survive. But a "talk time," she also knew, would help loving feelings blossom and with this form a special bond for the lovers who were caught up in a violent war and between two very different cultures. It was the best counsel that she could give the daughter she loved. It was a "tool" she believed in. Being committed to "happy talk" gave the couple a structure they could rely on, even at times when the war intruded.

Getting a handle on dealing with anger is the second "tool" that a growing couple cannot do without. And the best time to discuss and plan how to handle anger and conflicts is when neither partner is angry. Then, when the conflict comes, and it will if both partners are being honest, the plan is ready to be used.

Couples may try to avoid conflicts by withdrawing, placating, intimidation of various kinds, or lengthy explanations—all ineffective habits for handling anger—but all these techniques have their downsides and furthermore give no way to resolve the issue. Having an effective plan ready for use at the time of a disagreement is extremely helpful. *A creative use of conflict is a useful "tool" and makes the most identifiable impact on growth for the couple.*

An Experience with Further Development Through Organizations that Care about Healthy Marriage and Family

When a couple catches the value of the Maces' Primary Coping System, sees how it can strengthen marriages, and puts into practice its philosophies and ideals, one further step to take is to investigate the vehicles within the community which provide couples with various opportunities both to practice the skills that work and to teach them to others. In Fort Worth, Texas, where the Woods live, such a vehicle was developed through The Parenting Center, a non-profit organization with a big "garage," where many vehicles of aid to the Fort Worth community are housed.

Since there has been a movement in recent decades to provide preventive relationship work through federal grants, some of those money became available to a nonprofit coalition, hosted by The Parenting Center, called the Healthy Marriage/Healthy Family Coalition. Through grant funding, various programs such as PREP, Family Wellness, and "How to Avoid Marrying a Jerk(ette)" have provided training for couples to lead these selected programs in many training workshops in Tarrant County.

Two new programs developed from the training workshops:

- the Coalition-sponsored annual Healthy Marriage Conference, with well-known speakers and
- the MEG Date Nights, designed and led by the Woods. These sessions provide a positive refresher course for the Primary Coping System each month. At this writing, the MEG has been offered for six years and has served over 250 different couples.

The "timeless strengths" of the Maces' Primary Coping System are proved again and again as the Woods watch couples gain skills and confidence.

When couples are interested in leadership, the Woods recommend that they go through the training provided by Better Marriages in how to lead groups in couple growth. Very recently, four couples were trained to lead sessions and to start MEGs in cities adjacent to Fort Worth. The same foundation that funds the MEG Date Night provided the funds for these couples to be trained, and MEGs are multiplying. It is the continued hope that the number of couple leaders will grow, and more organizations will see the need for MEG sessions for couples helping their relationship in the midst of a busy life.

The more the couples stay in touch with the MEG Date Night, the more likely they will use the skills learned there. Many couples return after an absence to say that they need help with a "refresher," and they are grateful to have a place that exists just for that help. On a recent evaluation, one participant was asked why he returned, and he wrote just one word: "Pain." When that same participant was asked what he got out of the session, he wrote, "Ease from pain." It was a beautiful and very telling response to what happens when couples continue to be both honest and affirming with each other.

What is needed in every community is a small group of trained couples who can become the catalysts for the health of relationships in that community. Working within existing organizations, such as churches, non-profits, and organizations concerned with marriage and family (such as Better Marriages), provides a specific population to introduce the concept of the Primary Coping System and the MEG structure for involvement with other couples who want good things for their relationship.

It is a win/win/WIN accomplishment and just what the Maces had in mind all those decades ago.

On the last afternoon of the interview with the Maces, the Woods asked what three words each would say characterized their long and famous relationship. Each took the question seriously, took time to think, and then said:

Vera: *Trust* would be my first word. It has characterized our relationship from the very first meeting, and it is still important today. We trust each other to give the support we each need and to do the same with encouragement and affirmation. Trust needs to be present for a truly intimate relationship.

David: *Affirmation* would be an important one for me. Nobody in my life has affirmed me like Vera, and it has made a great difference.

The second would be *loyalty.*

Then *growth,* even growing through anger and disagreement. I think there was a great deepening of our love when we got anger licked.

When you close the door on the ugly things that you can say and do to each other, and you close it permanently, you open the door to a kind of growth that you did not realize would be possible.

Growth happened when we both recommitted our efforts to achieve it and growth continues today. It is the one thing that I am most appreciative of in our relationship.

Vera: I think *appreciation* is important too. I really appreciate David, and it is not a duty to tell him so. I want to. He is a great man and a loving husband, and I want him to be certain that is exactly what I believe. I tell him often.

The third characteristic of our relationship is *gratitude.* I am grateful for our years together and for the companionship or friendship that we have. We started as friends, and we have stayed friends throughout our long relationship.

David: I am so grateful for Vera, too. I think of how I have grown as a person, how I have changed and developed, and it's in large part due to her. She has encouraged me to grow as a person, and this, in turn, has sparked growth in our marriage relationship. I have learned to share myself with her, and it has led us to great heights of joy and understanding.

And today? I would say there has been no time up until now when we have been closer and happier. We are serene about our relationship.

Vera: I like the word serene. It suggests to me that you've passed through troubled waters and sailed into a safe and comfortable harbor. Why do you think we are now serene?

David: I think it's partly because we have accomplished most of our goals. That is both in terms of our careers and of our relationship. There is not much that we have left uncompleted or undone. By that I mean there is no bugle calling us to climb some new summit.

Vera: But you are talking about the external world of outside achievements. I want to talk about the internal world. Those achievements are wonderful, but I want to talk about that state of serenity. I think it means that we have worked out a lifestyle over the years together that is deeply satisfying.

David: I agree, the internal state is very satisfying. But it also says that we have achieved in making known to others the steps that have brought this relationship to such a place. We have continued to work on our relationship, to pursue growth in connection and closeness—and here we are. I am happy you like the concept of serenity; I want to call it an accomplishment.

Just to illustrate the impact of the Maces' work throughout the world, here is a partial list of the organizations with whom they worked, the institutions they served, and some of the many awards they received:

July 26, 1933—David and Vera were married in London.
May 19, 1938—David was one of the founders of the Marriage Guidance Council in London, with Marjorie Hume as Secretary. (*This was the first organization in the world designed specifically to help marriages.*)
October 1942—David became the Secretary of the Marriage Guidance Council. The other pioneers in this effort included: Dr. Herbert Gray, a Presbyterian minister, Dr. Ethel Dukes, an M.D. specialist in child guidance, Edward Griffith, M.D., Lilias Blackett Jeffries, gynecologist, and Joan Malleson, a gynecologist.
1943—Vera Mace returned to England from the US (where she had taken their daughters to safety) in order to work with David in the Marriage Guidance Council.
1945—David and Vera began a Radio Talk Show with the British Broadcasting Company about marriage and family, a fifteen-minute show.
1945–1952—David had full-page articles in *The Star*, a daily London newspaper, on subjects of marriage and family.
1947—David was invited to New York to speak at the annual conference of the prestigious National Council of Family Relations for his work in England with the Marriage Guidance Council, an organization which he was instrumental in spreading to other European countries after WWII, as well as South Africa, India, and Australia.
1947—David was elected President of the International Union of Family Organization.
1947—After the Mace family moved to the US, David began to write columns called "Can This Marriage Be Saved?" for American magazines. Among them were *Woman's Home Companion*, *McCall's*, and *Readers Digest*.
1948—David was the speaker at the National Conference on Family Life (where he and Vera met and had tea with President Harry Truman and his wife Bess).
1948—The British government funded the Marriage Guidance Council, setting a model for other countries to follow, such as

Australia and South Africa. David negotiated this decision with the help of two former presidents of the organization, Lord Horder (the King's physician), Geoffrey Fisher (then Bishop of London, later Archbishop of Canterbury), and Samuel Courtauld. At this point, the name was changed to the Marriage Guidance Council of England and still later to Relate. That organization is now celebrating over eighty years in existence.

1948—David resigned from the Methodist ministry over a definition of what makes a clergy ministry.

1949—David became Professor of Human Relations, Drew University.

1951—David and Vera attended the first White House Conference on the Family.

1951—David served as president of the National Council on Family Relations.

1952—David was the speaker at the International Union of Family Organizations in Oxford, where due to his address on the issue of the need for aid to couples, he was appointed as president, an office he held for sixteen years. It was here that David said, "The core of the family is the marriage relationship. Many marriages are functioning poorly because no direct help is offered to couples."

1959—David became a professor at the University of Philadelphia Medical School.

1959—David became Professor of Family Study, School of Medicine, University of Pennsylvania.

1960—David and Vera traveled to the Soviet Union, writing a book about marriage there, as they did about many other cultures.

1960–1967—David and Vera became the executive directors of the American Association for Marriage Counselors (which later became AAMFT) and spent seven years rebuilding this organization until it was firmly established nationally.

1962—David and Vera conducted their first marriage enrichment retreat in Kirkridge, Pennsylvania.

1966—David and Vera were UNESCO conference speakers, New Delhi, India.

1967—David became Professor of Family Sociology, Bowman Gray School of Medicine, Wake Forest University, Winston-Salem, North Carolina.

1973—David and Vera founded the ACME in Winston-Salem, North Carolina, on their fortieth anniversary.

At retirement, David became Director of Marriage Enrichment training, School of Pastoral Care, North Carolina Baptist Hospital.

August 29, 1983—The Maces received a personal note of congratulations from President Ronald Reagan and his wife Nancy on the occasion of their fiftieth anniversary.

1990—David Robert Mace died December 1.

1994—*David and Vera were recipients of the International Year of the Family Patron Award, given by the United Nations.*

In her acceptance speech of the award, Vera spoke of their work over the years and quoted Teilhard de Chardin about "harnessing . . . the active energies of love."

1994—In Australia, the National Marriage Guidance Council changed its name to Relationships Australia, Inc.

2008—Vera Chapman Mace died at age 106 on July 22.

The Maces received awards from the World Health Organization, the World Council of Churches, the International Union of Family Organizations, and many universities throughout the world.

They were also speakers and received awards at the Groves Conference, the Masters and Johnson conferences, the Sex Information and Education Council of the US, and the American Association of Sex Educators, Counselors, and Therapists.

David earned four degrees, a Bachelor of Science, a Bachelor of Arts and a Master of Arts from Cambridge University, and a Doctor of Philosophy from Manchester University.

Vera held a Bachelor of Science degree and a Master of Arts from Drew University. Both held honorary Doctor of Humanities degrees.

In spite of their many accolades and awards, the Maces' ideals are simple, as befitted a Quaker couple. At the heart of their philosophy of marriage is the sturdy belief that many couples continue to value their relationship throughout their lives and want it to flourish. They were committed throughout their lives to the idea of "building better marriages, beginning with our own."

There is an old aphorism about seeds and their importance. It says that you can count the number of seeds in an apple, but you can never count the number of apples in a seed. That saying suggests that there are countless numbers of couples around the world who have already profited from the Maces' Primary Coping System, and thus, the information is but a reminder of the valuable lessons they and their families have already learned. However, it is with great hope that many more couples will join in, scattering these seeds and seriously considering that that *impact on the future of our world is too important to wait another minute.*

The Maces were pioneers in a new field—the marriage relationship. The Maces began work in that new field in a time when the world was in turmoil (the Great Depression and WWII). They continued that work through the chaotic decades of the 1960s and 1970s, through social revolutions such as Civil Rights, Women's Liberation, Black Panthers, Students for a Democratic Society, Gay and Lesbian Rights, and cultural upheavals of various kinds, all of which led to a divorce rate that hovered around 50% and suggested that marriage was at best irrelevant and at worst doomed to failure for at least half of all those who tried it.

The Maces dared to propose *that the institution of marriage can bring order to the world by stabilizing and enriching the world's most basic relationship.* The Maces were optimistic, courageous, and wise. They were dreamers, yes, but throughout their lives they brought substance to their dreams and demonstrated as a couple every teaching and philosophy that they advised. They gave their ideas away, with the hope that others would find them helpful and carry them on. For the Woods, and countless other couples, the world is a better place because of David and Vera Mace.

Resources

A Map for Marriage: Before You Say I Do. Salida, CA: Family Wellness Associates, 2009.

Anderson, Claire. "Divorce Rates Drop to their Lowest Levels in Nearly 30 Years," *Mail Online* (Sept. 22, 2018), pp. 1–2.

Gottman, John. *Why Marriages Succeed or Fail.* New York: Simon and Schuster, 1994.

Heitler, Susan M. *Conflict to Resolution.* New York: W. W. Norton & Co., 1990.

Levinson, Robert. "Your Sex Life," *AARP Magazine* (May, 2018), p. 42.

Mace, David and Vera. *Better Marriages for a Better World.* Unpublished Manuscript, 1985.

Markman, H., Stanley, S., and Blumberg, S. *Fighting FOR Your Marriage.* San Francisco, CA: Jossey-Bass, 2001.

Miller, S. and Miller, P. *Couple Communication II, Thriving Together.* Evergreen, CO: Interpersonal Communications Programs, 1995.

Olson, David H. and Olson, Amy K. *Empowering Couples.* Minneapolis, MN: Life Innovations, Inc., 2000.

Sifferlin, Alexandra. "How Family Ties Keep You Going in Sickness and in Health," *Time* (Feb. 13, 2017), p. 20.

Stanley, Scott. *The Heart of Commitment.* Nashville, TN: Thomas Nelson Publishers, 2001.

Van Epp, John. *Becoming Better Together.* San Clemente, CA, 2017.

Wallerstein, Judith S. and Blakeslee, Sandra. *The Good Marriage.* New York: Warner Books, 1995.

Within Our Reach, Participant Workbook, Version 2.0. Greenwood Village, CO: PREP Educational Products, 2008.

Wood, Bobbye and Britton. *Marriage for the Everyday*. Franklin, TN: Carpenter's Son Publishing, 2017.

Books to Consider by the Maces

Close companions
Getting Ready for Marriage
How to Have a Happy Marriage
In the Presence of God: Readings for Christian Marriage
Letters to a Retired Couple: Marriage in the Later Years
Love and Anger in Marriage
Marriage East and West
Marriage Enrichment in the Church
Marriage Enrichment Retreats: Story of a Quaker Project
Men, Women, and God
Prevention in Family Services: Approaches to Family Wellness
The Sacred Fire: Christian Marriage through the Ages
The Soviet Family: Love, Marriage, Parenthood, and Family Life under Communism
We Can Have Better Marriages If We Really Want Them
What's Happening to Clergy Marriages
Whom God Hath Joined

Books to Consider by Britton and Bobbye Wood

Britton and Bobbye

Building Lasting Relationships
Christian Families Growing Stronger
Marriage for the Everyday: 365 Conversation Starters Designed to Deepen Couple Relationships
Marriage Readiness

Britton

The Experience of Grief: Reluctant Learning and Forced Growth
Single Adults Want to be the Church, Too
Survival KIT for Griefwork

Bobbye

Building Lasting Marriages

Acknowledgments

Thanks to our extraordinary close family for their encouragement to stay connected and grounded during life's shifting experiences.

Thanks to all those couples in Marriage Enrichment who inspired our early goals and offered realistic models and ideals for what could be achieved: David and Vera Mace, David and Sarah Catron, Genie and Preston Dyer, Cliff and Jane Ives, Jan and Mike Lundy, Eleanor and Gerald Roller, Bea and Jim Strickland, Jim and Johnne Armentrout, Bill and Linda McConahey, Chris and Ron Musgrave, Al and Carole Pugsley, Gerlinde and Ian Spencer, Bob and Lane Powell, Robert and Sally Chang, and many others.

Thanks to all the many friends and family members who gave us suggestions, their time and energy, specifically Bill Coffin and our daughter, Leigh Ann Wood Nicas.

Also, thanks to Greg and Priscilla Hunt, who have for many years led the Association for Couples in Marriage Enrichment (once called ACME and now called Better Marriages) and continued to produce and direct the IMEC begun in 1996 by Britton.

Thanks once again to Jesse and M.K. Larson for their support and belief:

- in the importance of MEGs to many churches and communities,
- in the importance to couples of the annual Healthy Marriage Conference in the Fort Worth/Dallas area with topics and speakers relevant to daily growth and marital enjoyment,
- in the helpfulness to couples everywhere of realistic books on the marriage relationship,
- and most of all in the concept that modern couples can profit from the relevance of the Mace's Primary Coping System and use it to increase the strength of families everywhere.

A personal word of gratitude to the Maces for their gifts to the world and to Bobbye and Britton as mentors, colleagues, and friends. The Maces were far ahead of their time as they encouraged an egalitarian approach in marriage, that as partners and companions the couple is to work together as a team.

We both learned so much from them as they came to Fort Worth, researched their book on *Close Companions*, and led a large Couple Retreat with seventy-two couples at the church where Britton was on staff. Seven MEGs were formed from that one experience.

When Britton considered going back to school to get his Ph.D. at age fifty, the Maces counseled him regarding whether to prepare as a family therapist or as a family life educator. They thought a family life educator had a greater longevity and a broader perspective in the enrichment field.

Britton enjoyed the experiences with the Maces in the National Council on Family Relations where David was an earlier president and often conveyed the marriage enrichment concepts. As the Maces walked down the hall, people would stop to talk with them, eventually as many as thirty or forty.

Even today, as Bobbye and Britton are in their eighties, Britton dreams of organizing a truly international conference that hosts all the marriage education programs and institutions from around the world, including representatives from all the organizations that the Maces helped to start. The purpose of the conference would be to talk about quality marriage, its place in every nation and every culture, and its impact on bringing peace in the world.

As David Mace said, "In order to achieve the companionship family, we must first make the companionship marriage work. That is the vital key to the building of a truly democratic society. *For this reason, the promotion of effective marriage enrichment on a large scale becomes a task of the first magnitude.*"